BEETHOVEN IN BEIJING

With forewords by

Philadelphia Orchestra Music Director **Yannick Nézet-Séguin**

and Retired U.S. Ambassador **Nicholas Platt**

BEETHOVEN
IN BEIJING

Stories from the Philadelphia Orchestra's
Historic Journey to China

JENNIFER LIN

TEMPLE UNIVERSITY PRESS *Philadelphia | Rome | Tokyo*

TEMPLE UNIVERSITY PRESS
Philadelphia, Pennsylvania 19122
tupress.temple.edu

Text design by Kate Nichols

Library of Congress Cataloging-in-Publication Data

Names: Lin, Jennifer, 1959– author. | Nézet-Séguin, Yannick, 1975– writer
    of foreword. | Platt, Nicholas, writer of foreword.
Title: Beethoven in Beijing : stories from the Philadelphia Orchestra's
    historic journey to China / Jennifer Lin ; with forewords by Philadelphia
    Orchestra Music Director Yannick Nézet-Séguin and Retired U.S.
    Ambassador Nicholas Platt.
Description: Philadelphia : Temple University Press, 2022. | Includes
    bibliographical references and index. | Summary: "An oral history of the
    first performances by an American orchestra in the People's Republic of
    China"—Provided by publisher.
Identifiers: LCCN 2021036953 | ISBN 9781439921616 (cloth)
Subjects: LCSH: Philadelphia Orchestra—Travel—China. | Concert
    tours—China. | Music and diplomacy—China. | Cultural diplomacy—China.
    | Cultural diplomacy—United States. | LCGFT: Oral histories.
Classification: LCC ML28.P5 P629 2022 | DDC 784.206/051—dc23
LC record available at https://lccn.loc.gov/2021036953

♾ The paper used in this publication meets the requirements of the American National
Standard for Information Sciences—Permanence of Paper for Printed Library Materials,
ANSI Z39.48–1992

Printed in the United States of America

9 8 7 6 5 4 3 2 1

To my husband, Bill, and our children, Karl and Cory:

With you, life is full of possibilities and joy.

Music produces a kind of pleasure

which human nature cannot do without.

—Confucius

CONTENTS

LIST OF CHARACTERS IN 1973

WHITE HOUSE:

Richard Nixon, president
Henry Kissinger, national security adviser

PHILADELPHIA ORCHESTRA:

Eugene Ormandy, conductor
Alan Abel, percussion
James Barnes, stagehand
Davyd Booth, violin
Robert de Pasquale, violin
Renard Edwards, viola
Daniel Epstein, guest pianist
Bernard Garfield, bassoon
Emilio Gravagno, double bass
Larry Grika, violin

Louis Hood, public relations
Julia Janson, violin
John Krell, piccolo
Herbert Light, violin
Margarita Csonka Montanaro, harp
Hai-ye Ni, cello
Anthony Orlando, percussion
Booker Rowe, violin
Edward Viner, tour physician
Judith Viner, tour nurse

CHINESE MUSICIANS:

Cui Zhuping, violin
Liu Qi, bassoon
Tan Dun, composer
Julia Tsien, piano

Yin Chengzong, piano
Zhang Dihe, oboe
Zhu Gongqi, violin

MEDIA:

Steve Bell, ABC News
Sandy Grady, the *Philadelphia Bulletin*
Kati Marton, WCAU-TV
Harold Schonberg, the *New York Times*
Daniel Webster, the *Philadelphia Inquirer*

OTHER:

John Holdridge, U.S. Liaison Office, Beijing, deputy chief
Nicholas Platt, U.S. Liaison Office, Beijing, political officer
Sheila Platt, wife of Nicholas Platt
Francis Tenny, U.S. State Department, cultural affairs officer

FOREWORD

Yannick Nézet-Séguin
Music Director
The Philadelphia Orchestra

Music Director Yannick Nézet-Séguin first toured China with the Philadelphia Orchestra in 2014. (Photo by Jan Regan.)

Music, of course, is at the heart of any international tour of the Philadelphia Orchestra. It is always thrilling to perform to sold-out crowds at the spectacular National Centre for the Performing Arts in Beijing, at the dazzling Shanghai Oriental Art Center, or at halls in Tianjin (Philadelphia's sister city), Shenzhen, and Changsha, to name just a few. But some of my fondest memories are of the activities that bring us closer to the young musicians and communities of China.

Whenever the Philadelphia Orchestra travels, there is always an element of cultural exchange, especially in China, where our history as the first American orchestra to visit, in 1973, is remembered and revered as an early and much-appreciated gesture of friendship. Today, we cultivate and plan activities that we describe as people-to-people exchanges. This approach—independent of any political aspects—is part of the orchestra's DNA, and I think it reflects a singular Philadelphia spirit.

Whether giving master classes, performing side-by-side with students, surprising audiences with pop-up concerts, or participating in the China International Music Competition, we have a rich tradition of engagement beyond the concert hall in educational institutions and civic settings.

I will never forget our visit, in partnership with the U.S. Embassy in Beijing, to Minzu University, the only university in China where all of the country's fifty-six ethnic groups are represented in the faculty and student body. During this beautiful and unique opportunity for musical exchange, students taught orchestra members Chinese folk tunes, and we heard performances on traditional Mongolian instruments, including the horsehead fiddle. We all performed together—across culture, language, and musical style, yet united in music. I will always treasure this memory.

At the Philadelphia Orchestra, we like to say that music is an equalizing force that gives voice to ideas and emotions that words alone cannot. Today, as I write in these difficult times, it is ever more important to continue doing our work. We look forward to continuing to create joy, connection, and excitement through music around the world. And we are grateful that our long-standing history with the people of China is richly documented in this book.

FOREWORD

NICHOLAS PLATT
Ambassador of the United States, retired

This book explains how the Philadelphia Orchestra became a household name in China in 1973. It still is. The orchestra has returned to China again and again, forging lasting collaborations with orchestras and media outlets in several of China's major cities as well as in smaller ones. In each city, performances are combined with people-to-people exchanges, such as pop-up concerts, side-by-side performances with local ensembles, and residency programs, including master classes, instruction at conservatories and schools, and lectures in arts administration.

Relations between the United States and the People's Republic of China had two beginnings. First came Richard Nixon's visit in February 1972, which started contact between the governments in Washington, DC, and Beijing and reset the world balance of power. The second occurred the following year with exchanges between private institutions and individuals, including American bankers, traders, lawmakers, manufacturers, swimmers, basketball players, scientists—and the Philadelphia Orchestra.

Diplomat Nicholas Platt with Chinese Premier Zhou Enlai in 1973 after Platt joined the new U.S. Liaison Office in Beijing. (Courtesy of Nicholas Platt.)

As a U.S. State Department foreign service officer at the time, I took part in the Nixon visit and in the door-opening exchanges. They were entirely different events. Nixon's visit was formal and meticulously controlled, with our Chinese hosts nervously avoiding unscripted contact between us and ordinary people. But the visit by the Philadelphia Orchestra in September 1973 stands out for its lasting impact to this day. I was stationed at the newly opened U.S. Liaison Office in Beijing and had negotiated arrangements for the visit. My wife and I were assigned to take care of Conductor Eugene Ormandy and his wife, Gretel, giving us a front-row seat for the entire tour. Chairman Mao Zedong's wife, Jiang Qing, who was known in the West as Madame Mao, had control over culture, which made the orchestra's every move carefully scrutinized and fraught with political risk.

China has become a major market for Western classical music. While other world orchestras and conservatories have developed lasting relationships in China, no other American orchestra is delivering the depth and breadth of programming in China as the Philadelphia Orchestra, and none has a longer relationship.

At a time when growing tension and disagreement mark other aspects of the U.S.-China relationship, cooperation in the world of music is gaining momentum. It's a very big, very complicated relationship. But, like the weather, it's different at different levels. When you are up in the high altitude, it can be cold. The winds blow hard. But when you get down closer to the surface of the earth, where the weather is warmer, the relationship is totally flourishing, particularly inside the concert hall.

A NOTE ON REPORTING, SPELLING, AND ORGANIZATION

Before writing this book, I made a documentary by the same name with Sam Katz, founder of History Making Productions, and codirected with Sharon Mullally. Many of the quotes here are taken from interviews or research for the film. For this book, however, I went deeper and included commentary from personal journals, newspaper accounts from reporters on tour, memoirs, and archival audio recordings. I also quote from diplomatic cables between the U.S. Liaison Office in Beijing and the U.S. State Department in Washington, DC, that I accessed through WikiLeaks. As an oral history, I provide details on each commentator in the end notes, explaining the source of the information and whether it is a statement from an interview, an excerpt from a personal journal, or a quote from a news account.

With the spelling of places and people in China, I default to contemporary pinyin spellings. For example, I use Yin Chengzong for the Chinese pianist who performed with the Philadelphia Orchestra, instead of an older version of his name—Yin Cheng-chung—that was used in diplomatic cables in 1973. There are some exceptions. For some historical figures, I default to the spelling most known by the public, such as Chiang Kai-shek for the former president of the Republic of China. Also, given that this is an oral history, I retain the use of Peking and not Beijing in diplomatic cables from 1973 or when a person speaking at that time refers to the capital.

BEETHOVEN IN BEIJING

INTRODUCTION

This journey into the past started with a reporting assignment for the *Philadelphia Inquirer*. In 2008, the Philadelphia Orchestra was touring China and marking the thirty-fifth anniversary of its groundbreaking 1973 tour with a special concert in Beijing. The paper's music critics could not make the trip, so the editors sent me. My knowledge of classical music was shallow, but as a former China correspondent for the *Inquirer* in the 1990s, I knew my way around. To gauge China's classical music scene at the time, I reported stories from around the country. I tracked down the Chinese pianist Yin Chengzong, one of the composers of the *Yellow River Concerto*, who also performed it with the orchestra in 1973. I spent a day interviewing him at his family's historic villa on the island of Gulangyu in the southern province of Fujian. I went to a piano school in Beijing to talk to teachers and parents about the burgeoning interest in studying such instruments as the piano and the violin. On the night of the concert, held in the same venue as the 1973 performances, I interviewed Chinese concertgoers before and after the anniversary concert, and I was struck by the sincere, deep nostalgia that people had for the orchestra. Many older patrons shared with great fondness and clarity their recollections of the groundbreaking 1973 visit. As Nicholas Platt explains in his foreword, the Philadelphia Orchestra was a household name in China. How did I not know this? I had lived and worked in China in the 1990s, but my travels did not take me into many concert halls. If I was unaware of this lasting affection for my hometown orchestra, surely others were as well.

I covered the anniversary concert, featuring the remarkable Lang Lang performing the *Yellow River Concerto* as Yin Chengzong listened from the audience. Returning home, I was convinced that this story not only should be read but heard and seen. I pitched the idea of a documentary to the orchestra in 2015, and, a year later, Sam Katz, the visionary filmmaker behind History Making Productions, agreed to work with me to launch the making of the film. Within months, we were off to China, covering the orchestra's 2016 tour in Shanghai and Beijing, which featured guest artist Lang Lang.

In writing the script, I learned that building a visual story requires a different set of skills and discipline. I did not have the luxury of letting anecdotes ramble or taking detours with the narrative. As they say, so much material was left on the metaphorical cutting-room floor of the edit room. When the coronavirus swept across the United States in March 2020 and we were forced to quarantine, I saw the months of isolation as an opportunity to turn the hours and hours of untapped material into a book. I wanted to focus the lens on the 1973 tour, the starting point for the orchestra's nearly half century of involvement in China and a forgotten chapter in the history of U.S.-China relations. The notion of "ping-pong diplomacy" is familiar to many, but music diplomacy arguably has left a more lasting legacy that resonates yet today. This book lets the women and men who lived that moment tell the story in their own words.

1 | OVERTURE

In his dressing room at the Academy of Music, Conductor Eugene Ormandy began to unwind. It had been a long night—a two-and-a-half-hour marathon of Bach's monumental *Saint Matthew Passion* with a choir of two hundred before a full house in the ornate concert hall. Next week, it would be more of the same when Maestro Ormandy performed the concert as the finale for the Philadelphia Orchestra's annual New York season.

But on this night, Ormandy had something else on his mind—geopolitics. All week long, he had read and heard about an improbable turn of events in relations between the United States and China. A U.S. table tennis team, which had been competing at the world championship in Japan, received an unexpected, last-minute invitation to visit Beijing. The fifteen athletes accepted and, just like that, became the first American group of any kind invited to mainland China since 1949.

Just days earlier, a headline on the front page of the *Philadelphia Inquirer* declared, "After 22 Years, Americans Are Welcome in China." A correspondent for the Associated Press swooned, "The spring-like warmth in U.S.-China contacts at the human level cannot fail to melt some of the ice that has congealed in the long winter of hostility."

Over the course of the visit, the reporter detailed where the athletes went (the Great Wall), whom they met (Premier Zhou Enlai), what they ate (an eight-course banquet, including shrimp with pigeon eggs), and, yes, how they played before a Beijing crowd of eighteen thousand (losses for both the American men and women).

Taking it all in, Ormandy mulled with more than a little envy all the fuss. "If a ping-pong team can go, why can't we?" he wondered aloud to the orchestra manager, Boris Sokoloff. "How would you get an invitation to China, Boris?"

President Richard Nixon and Eugene Ormandy at the Philadelphia Orchestra's annual gala on January 24, 1970. Nixon traveled by train to Philadelphia to present Ormandy with the Presidential Medal of Freedom. At left is the president of the Academy of Music, Stuart Louchheim.

(Photo courtesy of the Philadelphia Orchestra Association Archives, used with kind permission.)

"Let's write the White House," the manager offered. "Nixon's always liked the orchestra."

Indeed, in 1970, Richard Nixon and his wife, Pat, had traveled by Metroliner train to Philadelphia to award Ormandy the Presidential Medal of Freedom, the highest civilian honor in the country. Welcomed with "Hail to the Chief" as he entered the Prince of Wales box at the Academy of Music with the First Lady, Nixon was treated to his favorite, Tchaikovsky's "1812 Overture." For extra fanfare, the Valley Forge Military Academy Band joined the orchestra on stage.

Ormandy wasted no time in writing to the White House about China, but the reply was not the one that he wanted. Despite all the goodwill coming from "ping-pong diplomacy," the United States did not have official diplomatic relations with China, which meant there was no American embassy in Beijing and no Chinese embassy in Washington, DC. A White House aide suggested that Ormandy try reaching out to the nearest Chinese ambassador—in Ottawa, Canada. Ormandy did write, but the request went nowhere. Undeterred, he kept nudging his friends in high places to press his case.

The "winter of hostility" between China and the United States was in its third decade. The two countries had barely spoken to each other since the creation of the Communist People's Republic of China in 1949. The superpowers had been on opposite sides of wars in Korea and Vietnam and had severed full diplomatic relations. Any contact on such issues as prisoners of war had to be conducted through diplomats in a third-party country, Poland. And then there was the divisive matter of Taiwan. During China's civil war, the United States had sided with the Nationalist government, which retreated to the island of Taiwan after being defeated by the People's Liberation Army. As long as the United States stayed loyal to the Nationalists, relations with the mainland remained severed.

But in the spring of 1971, with table tennis in the news, a new reality was taking hold in both Washington and Beijing. Even before he became president, Nixon acknowledged that a foreign policy that excluded a fifth of all humans—in other words, China—did not make any sense at all. He wanted to normalize the diplomatic relationship and end decades of isolation.

China's leaders, meanwhile, were deeply suspicious of the Soviet Union. Contrary to popular perception, the Communist world was not a unified front, with the Chinese and the Soviets linked as comrades in arms. In fact, China was becoming increasingly worried about the possibility of a Soviet invasion. In the late 1960s, the Soviets had built up forces along the Chinese border. China viewed the United States as a potential foil to Soviet aggression. Nixon, meanwhile, realized that reaching out to Chairman Mao Zedong could put the head of the Soviet Union, Leonid Brezhnev, off balance.

The invitation to the ping-pong players was a tentative first step. Nicholas Platt, a China expert at the State Department at the time, framed the visit this way: "The Chinese wanted to send a message to the United States that they were willing to talk. The Chinese started to wink at the United States—and the United States winked back."

In less than a year's time, the winking led to a historic meeting in February 1972, when Nixon traveled to snowy Beijing to meet Chairman Mao and Premier Zhou. China's

President Nixon, upon arriving in Beijing, joins Chinese Premier Zhou Enlai in reviewing troops. (Courtesy of the Richard Nixon Presidential Library and Museum/National Archives and Records Administration.)

state-controlled media declared that this visit was a good thing. For the first time in years, Chinese people could openly express curiosity about Americans—interest that previously would have been grounds for punishment or retribution.

Delegations of athletes, including American swimmers, divers, and college basketball players, were invited to China, as were groups of scientists, physicians, archaeologists, teachers, psychologists, and members of Congress. In Ormandy's corner was the powerful Republican senator from Philadelphia, Minority Leader Hugh Scott, who brought up the Philadelphia Orchestra when he met the premier during a Senate trip to China in April 1972.

But Zhou was one step ahead of him. The premier had already begun using cultural exchanges, particularly with European classical musicians, to expose the Chinese public to Western culture and to soften negative perceptions that had hardened over the decades.

A table-tennis exhibition by China's national team, attended by President Nixon and his entourage on their 1972 visit. The year before, an American team had played in China—a visit dubbed as "ping-pong diplomacy" that helped open the doors of diplomacy between the nations. (Courtesy of the Richard Nixon Presidential Library and Museum/National Archives and Records Administration.)

Under Mao, a generation of Chinese had been raised to think of America as public enemy number one. In 1972, as part of "music diplomacy," Zhou invited the renowned London Philharmonic and Vienna Philharmonic to perform in China. But his real goal was diplomatic, and his priority was improving relations with the United States.

And for that, he wanted an American orchestra.

In February 1973, the premier met with National Security Adviser Henry Kissinger, who was on a swing through Asia to advance peace talks to end the Vietnam War. The topic of more cultural exchanges came up. By now, Zhou had made up his mind. He would invite the Philadelphia Orchestra to be the first American orchestra to perform in mainland China.

From the perspective of nearly a half century later, what transpired next looms as a watershed event in the cultural histories of the two nations and in the personal lives of the people

Nixon and his entourage at the Great Wall in 1972. During the visit, he declared, "One result of this trip we hope may be that walls erected, whether physical like this one, or whether they are other walls, ideological or philosophical, will not divide the people of the world." (Courtesy of the Richard Nixon Presidential Library and Museum/ National Archives and Records Administration.)

involved. Our present-day cynicism inclines us to reject the sentimental notion of music as a bridge between people, of art and culture as diplomacy. But at that time, the propaganda-fueled suspicion and wariness between the nations was undeniable—as was the mutual good-will of those who performed and connected during the trip, however briefly.

The timing of the ten-day visit in September 1973 elevated its significance. From a foreign-policy standpoint, even after the Nixon meeting and the increasing willingness of China to invite delegations from the United States, no one could say with certainty where China was heading. In early 1973, diplomats in the newly opened United States Liaison Office in Beijing (then called Peking by Westerners) still had to rely on reading the tea leaves to divine the palace intrigue among China's leaders. The competing camps pitted Premier Zhou against Mao's powerful fourth wife, Jiang Qing, the leader of what would later be disparaged as the notorious Gang of Four. In the days before, during, and after the Philadelphia Orchestra's trip, U.S. foreign service officers shared classified cables deconstructing every gesture, every interaction, every utterance for meaning. Even Madame Mao's fashion choice at a concert—a Western-style black dress accented with white pumps and a white handbag—warranted a mention in a diplomatic cable from Beijing to the U.S. State Department.

On a broader scale, the tour offered insight into where China was in terms of the Cultural Revolution, a chaotic, repressive period of political upheaval, launched by Mao in 1966 to stoke revolutionary embers. The slogan of the Cultural Revolution was "Destroy the old to build the new." Western culture was reviled as bourgeois to the point that Chinese musicians were banned from performing the works of such classical composers as Beethoven and Mozart. The first few years, from 1966 to 1970, were the most violent. Many lives were destroyed, particularly those of artists, musicians, and intellectuals, whom young Red Guards viewed as emblematic of old ways. With Mao's tacit approval, mobs attacked, publicly humiliated, and sometimes summarily executed their victims. No one knows the real number of fatalities during this period, but estimates range from hundreds of thousands to more than a million. The number of lives disrupted and careers ruined is incalculable.

Mao deemed that art served politics and that the only acceptable forms of entertainment—an area that fell under the control of his wife—were operas, ballets, and symphonies with revolutionary themes. Against this backdrop, the idea of China hosting some of the greatest orchestras in the world was a clear signal of a changing direction. But how far would Zhou's music diplomacy go? Would the premier prevail? Or his nemesis, Madame Mao?

Ormandy would call the orchestra's tour of China "bigger than music." The American musicians, accustomed to international travel, had experienced nothing like it and sensed history in the making. Chinese musicians and audiences, who had longed to hear Western music again, would later describe the artistic and emotional impact of the concerts. After the orchestra departed China, however, the political winds suddenly shifted, dealing a setback to music diplomacy with a synchronized attack in state media against Beethoven. Not until Mao's death in 1976, which marked the definitive end to the Cultural Revolution, were the

The revolutionary ballet *The Red Detachment of Women* was performed in Shanghai for President Nixon. In the ballet, one of the limited number of productions approved for Chinese audiences, a housemaid is abused by a warlord and joins a revolutionary troop of women soldiers. (Courtesy of the Richard Nixon Presidential Library and Museum/National Archives and Records Administration.)

restrictions on classical music lifted, allowing Chinese musicians to freely pursue training and resume performing works by the great composers.

In looking back at the visit by the Philadelphia Orchestra, diplomats and historians can detect glimmers of a cultural reawakening that would reach full flower in succeeding generations. And the enduring legacy of this rebirth is seen now in the legions of music students in China and the number of new professional orchestras, conservatories, and first-class concert halls as well as Chinese musicians in orchestras around the world.

"It was ten of the most intense days of my life," recalls Kati Marton, the lone television reporter to accompany the orchestra on tour.

To understand the prevailing mind-set at that moment in history—and the subsequent thaw and bloom—we need to listen to the voices of those who lived it.

Here is what they said.

On January 20, 1973, Richard Nixon was inaugurated for his second term. In a break from tradition, he honored Eugene Ormandy by requesting that the Philadelphia Orchestra perform at a concert at the Kennedy Center. It was interpreted as an overt snub of the National Symphony Orchestra, the hometown orchestra in Washington, DC, which was accustomed to carrying out inauguration duties. In Philadelphia, there also was backlash. A few musicians did not want to perform, protesting Nixon's handling of the Vietnam War. The inauguration appearance was, as Boris Sokoloff, the orchestra manager, told the Associated Press, "a political nightmare." But it paid dividends for Ormandy. A month later—February 20, 1973—the conductor was nursing a cold in his apartment at the Barclay Hotel on Rittenhouse Square, when the phone rang at 4:46 P.M. An operator told Ormandy that the president wished to talk to him. "Which president?" Maestro Ormandy asked. The one in the White House, he was told.

President Richard Nixon: Mr. Ormandy?

Ormandy: How are you, Mr. President?

Nixon: How are you?

Ormandy: Thank you. A little sick. Otherwise, I'm fine.

Nixon: I'm just sitting here talking to Dr. [Henry] Kissinger. He's just back from China.

Ormandy: I know.

President Richard Nixon and Henry Kissinger, his assistant for National Security Affairs, in the Oval Office. On February 20, 1973, when Nixon called Conductor Eugene Ormandy about an invitation to tour China, Kissinger had just returned from meetings in Beijing with Chairman Mao Zedong and Premier Zhou Enlai. During that visit, they negotiated the opening of a U.S. Liaison Office in Beijing, matched with a Chinese office in Washington, DC. (Courtesy of the Richard Nixon Presidential Library and Museum/National Archives and Records Administration.)

Nixon: I thought you'd be interested to know when he was talking to our friends in China, Mr. Zhou Enlai—now, this has to be held 'til Thursday, but I thought you'd like to know—they're going to invite the Philadelphia Symphony to come to China.

Ormandy: That's wonderful.

Nixon: So, I just want you to know that my favorite symphony will be the first one to go to China. It will be a great experience for all of your people.

Ormandy: It's a great honor.

Nixon: I think it must have embarrassed you a little when some of them didn't want you to play at my inauguration. Now that the war is over, they probably feel a little bad about it. But you stood up to them.

Ormandy: Mr. President, you honor me. You honor the orchestra. I'm very proud and happy.

Nixon: We're most appreciative. I'll let Dr. Kissinger tell you about the conversation . . . would you like to hear about it?

Ormandy: If I may?

Nixon: Here he is.

Henry Kissinger, national security adviser: Mr. Ormandy?

Ormandy: Hello, Dr. Kissinger.

Kissinger: Nice to talk to you. I was talking to the Chinese leaders about exchanges, and they said to me the president had taken such a special interest in the Philadelphia Symphony, that he had taken a trip to Philadelphia once, and you agreed to play at the inauguration. So, the first Western symphony orchestra to come to China should be the Philadelphia Symphony.

Even though Richard Nixon had gotten the name slightly wrong (it's not the "Philadelphia Symphony"), the president had a fondness for Eugene Ormandy and the orchestra that reached back to his youth, when he listened to albums recorded by the Philadelphians.

Emilio Gravagno, double bass: Ormandy had taken over from the great conductor Leopold Stokowski [co-conducting from 1936]. Ormandy was a very fine, intuitive conductor. But I don't think he quite reached the pinnacle of reputation that Stokowski had prior to him. At that time, Ormandy was considered more of a caretaker of the orchestra. He kept the orchestra in good shape from the way Stokowski had left it.

Alan Abel, percussion: He was a violinist, so he was very aware of the strings and really got the strings to play big and lush and beautifully. He really felt the music. When I was first in the orchestra, we were held back a little bit, the brass and percussion sections.

Gravagno: We were known for "The Philadelphia Sound." The Academy of Music had good acoustics, but they were a little bit lacking in holding the sound. As a result of that, the orchestra players were always encouraged to hold the notes a lot longer. We were playing longer bows. So, the sound had a longer, more *tenuto* quality.

Conductor Eugene Ormandy in rehearsal with the Philadelphia Orchestra. (Photo courtesy of the Philadelphia Orchestra Association Archives, used with kind permission.)

Opened in 1857, the Academy of Music on South Broad Street is the oldest opera house in the United States that is still used for its original purpose. It was home to the Philadelphia Orchestra until 2001, when the orchestra moved to the newly built Kimmel Center for the Performing Arts. (Photo courtesy of the Philadelphia Orchestra Association Archives, used with kind permission.)

Bernard Garfield, bassoon: It's a super-sensitive hall, where all the players had to play everything as precisely as the conductor required. It is not a large, booming hall, which eats up a lot of the instruments. Ormandy insisted that the instruments be blended. So, if you had a passage that involved flute, oboe, clarinet, and bassoon, he wanted them to match very well and not have one pushing out his sound. And that developed into a very velvety sound, which is what the orchestra is known for.

Davyd Booth, violin and keyboard: Ormandy was the last of these conductors who were basically very powerful, one-man dictators. I would not say that Ormandy was a man of musical genius; he was really a political genius in the full sense of the word. He loved the sense of power that came from associating with a United States president.

Margarita Csonka Montanaro, harp: I would have been shocked if Nixon had asked someone else to go to China.

Daniel Webster, music critic for the *Philadelphia Inquirer*: Playing at Nixon's inauguration gave the Philadelphia Orchestra a lot of visibility and was probably noticed in China. They may have thought, "Oh, they're the number-one orchestra if they're playing for the president of the United States."

Eugene Ormandy: Our orchestra has traveled more for artistic propaganda than any other orchestra in this country. We've been traveling since '55. We carry the torch for American music. The last time we were in Vienna, one of the top newspapers and a very famous music critic wrote, "Technical perfection—plus soul," as if it were something unusual for an American orchestra. It hurt me—I was really insulted because American orchestras have as much soul as any of them abroad. But we are known to be a country of technical machinery. We are not a machine, believe me, anything but.

Nicholas Platt, former U.S. foreign service officer in Beijing: Ormandy had a thing about the Philadelphia Orchestra being first at everything. Then, too, I think the Chinese accepted the idea of inviting the Philadelphia Orchestra because in 1940, at the Academy of Music, Ormandy and Stokowski held a benefit concert to aid China in its fight against Japan during World War II.

The Fabulous Philadelphians

On November 17, 1900, in an article tucked on page 3 of the *Philadelphia Inquirer* between ads for corsets, handkerchiefs, and opera glasses, a reviewer declared that the debut of the Philadelphia Orchestra at the Academy of Music "left something to be desired." But the reporter predicted that Conductor Fritz Scheel had organized an orchestra of which "Philadelphia may properly feel proud; one which we need not fear to put into comparison with any other, bar none." In time, the orchestra would rise to the ranks of the so-called Big Five, the best of the best in America, alongside orchestras from New York, Boston, Chicago, and Cleveland. The "Fabulous Philadelphians," as hometown boosters dubbed them, were noted for their artistry as well as an expansive library of recordings.

Leopold Stokowski, a conductor and organist who joined in 1912, was credited with creating the signature "Philadelphia Sound," a rich, swelling style that arose from the string sections' compensating for the dry acoustics of the Academy of Music. With a knack for showmanship, Stokowski expanded the repertoire to include more modern works, broadened the orchestra's appeal with such innovations as children's concerts, and brought the orchestra Hollywood fame. Who could forget the memorable scene from the 1940 animated Disney classic *Fantasia*, in which the wild-haired Stokowski stands before the Philadelphia Orchestra and, from the podium, shakes the hand of Mickey Mouse?

In 1936, Eugene Ormandy was brought in as co-conductor, taking over as music director in 1938. Over the decades, the Philadelphia Orchestra was so successful with its record sales that royalties kept the organization afloat. The first celebrity recording featured the composer and pianist Sergei Rachmaninoff, who would continue to record with the Philadelphians for more than a decade. Pianist Lang Lang listened to those recordings as a child in China, calling the albums featuring the composer performing his own music "like God-given gifts."

In 1984, at the age of eighty-four, Ormandy performed his final concert at New York's Carnegie Hall. It curiously featured Beethoven's Sixth Symphony, the *Pastoral*, the source of so much consternation between the conductor and Jiang Qing in China in 1973. Following him at the helm of the Philadelphia Orchestra were Ricardo Muti, Wolfgang Sawallisch, Christoph Eschenbach, Charles Dutoit, and Yannick Nézet-Séguin.

An Expression of Appreciation

◆

A pebble is tossed into the serene water of a quiet lake. A ripple stirs, a small circle, then wider and wider it grows until almost imperceptibly millions of drops have been moved because of it.

So will be the far-reaching effect of this evening of music in Philadelphia.

The pages of this program will tell you something of the work we are trying to accomplish; of the rehabilitation needed; the aid given toward the maintenance of war orphanages; the little crippled children cared for in China's first Orthopaedic Hospital; refugee work carried on.

To each one of you, who has so splendidly and generously offered his services this evening, we give our heartfelt thanks. To Mr. Ormandy, Mr. Stokowski, Mr. Caston, Mr. O'Connell; to Miss Rose Bampton, Mr. Emanuel Feuermann, Mr. Joseph Szigeti, Mr. Alexander Kipnis; to each individual member of the great Philadelphia Orchestra; to each musician from the Curtis Institute of Music; to the American Federation of Musicians, Local 77; to Mr. John Frederick Lewis, President of The Academy of Music; and to the patrons, patronesses and guests who by their presence, have made this evening a success—we give our gratitude and appreciation.

From the storehouse of your hearts you have given much. It will never be forgotten.

CHINA AID COUNCIL

PROGRAM

CHINA AID CONCERT
ACADEMY OF MUSIC
MARCH 21, 1940

• • •

CONDUCTORS

LEOPOLD STOKOWSKI   EUGENE ORMANDY
SAUL CASTON   CHARLES O'CONNELL

ORCHESTRA

MEMBERS OF PHILADELPHIA ORCHESTRA
AND
CURTIS INSTITUTE OF MUSIC

SOLOISTS

ROSE BAMPTON . . . . *Soprano*
EMANUEL FEUERMANN . . . . *Violoncellist*
JOSEPH SZIGETI . . . . *Violinist*
ALEXANDER KIPNIS . . . . *Baritone*

• • •

Proceeds
1. China's First Orthopaedic Hospital in Kweiyang
2. American Refugee Hospital in Shanghai
3. Chinese War Orphans
4. Refugee Rehabilitation in China

The program for the China Aid Concert at the Academy of Music on March 21, 1940. The concert, which featured Eugene Ormandy and Leopold Stokowski, left an indelible mark in the collective memory of the Chinese people. (Photo courtesy of the Philadelphia Orchestra Association Archives, used with kind permission.)

The concert had raised funds for medical service for China's Eighth Route Army, which had been supported by the Canadian physician Dr. Norman Bethune.

Webster: That benefit concert made a big impression. Everyone in China remembered it.

Gravagno: Another reason why we were in a particularly good position to be invited to go to China was the fact that Nixon had given Ormandy the Presidential Medal of Freedom in 1970 at the Academy of Music.

Larry Grika, violin: At that concert, we were doing Tchaikovsky's "1812 Overture," and the Secret Service went absolutely berserk. There was almost a confrontation. When you're playing the "1812 Overture," you use cannons. Well, you can't use cannons too easily at the Academy of Music unless you want to see holes in the walls. So, to make the sound, a percussionist had to fire a rifle with blanks into a barrel backstage. At rehearsal, Mickey Bookspan got ready to fire when he's collared by some Secret Service guy who screamed, "What are you doing with that rifle?! Do you know Nixon is going to be here tonight?!"

Abel: For the concert, with Nixon and his wife in a box seat, the Secret Service made us change how we made the cannon sound. We had to get a Philadelphia police officer to be the actual one firing the rifle. A Secret Service agent held the rifle, passed it to the policeman, and then a percussionist on stage would cue him, saying, "You, shoot! You, shoot! You, shoot!" When it was over, the Secret Service took the rifle away.

1940 China Aid Concert

The benefit concert for China in 1940 at the Academy of Music was part of a larger charm offensive by the leaders of the Republic of China to win friends and influence Americans. At the time, China was battling Japan, which, in 1937, had launched assaults on Beijing and Tianjin, bombed Nanjing, and occupied Shanghai. Despite the escalating war, the United States was reluctant to give President Chiang Kai-shek more military support. According to John Pomfret, author of *The Beautiful Country and the Middle Kingdom: America and China, 1776 to the Present* (Henry Holt, 2016), China's ambassador to Washington, DC, Hu Shih, traveled across the United States, giving talks and meeting with opinion-makers in an effort to turn American sympathy for China into concrete action and financial aid. "China is now at Valley Forge," Hu said at one event, "but I hope she will soon be at Yorktown!"

The PR blitz featured pilots Hilda Yan and Li Xiaqing flying from city to city in the *Spirit of New China* monoplane to spread goodwill, a special arrangement of the Republic of China's national anthem by bandleader Artie Shaw, black-tie fundraisers for China relief in such posh settings as New York's Hotel Pierre, and such concerts as the benefit hosted by the Philadelphia Orchestra and the Curtis Institute of Music on March 21, 1940. The program for the concert included heart-wrenching photos of homeless refugees and wounded orphans as well as a note of appreciation from Ambassador Hu. The China Aid Council wrote, "A pebble is tossed into the serene water of a quiet lake. A ripple stirs, a small circle, then wider and wider it grows until almost imperceptibly millions of drops have been moved because of it. So will be the far-reaching effect of this evening of music in Philadelphia."

Orchestra musicians typically knew tour stops and what they'd be performing a year in advance. Not so for the China tour. This was like no other trip, with Chinese officials at the highest levels controlling every aspect of the visit.

Daniel Webster: There was no such thing as having Orchestra Manager Boris Sokoloff sit down with a Chinese impresario [and] give him dates and a list of players, repertoire, and housing and travel needs. Communication was through shadowy diplomatic ties.

Nicholas Platt: The actual visit by the orchestra was preceded by months and months of negotiations on what should be played, where they should go, whom they should meet. This was my job. I had been part of Nixon's trip to China in 1972. A year later, I helped open the U.S. Liaison Office in Beijing, a precursor to a full embassy, which would not open until 1979.

Francis Tenny, U.S. State Department cultural affairs officer: The first need was to establish the dates for a two-week tour in the year 1973. The only free two-week period was early September, after the orchestra's annual August residence in Saratoga Springs, New York, and before the opening of the regular season in Philadelphia.

Platt: At the Chinese foreign ministry, we haggled endlessly over the details of the visit, negotiating music programs as if they were treaties. It was very tricky business because the wife of Mao, Jiang Qing, was in charge of culture—and hoped to be in charge of a lot of other things, including the entire country—and was a very terrifying figure. She had very firm ideas about what should be played and what should not.

Tenny: For months, there were no replies from China . . . nothing except, "Yes, the September dates are fine." It began to appear to Sokoloff and the maestro that they were expected to disappear into the unknown. The maestro was impatient, and in the absence of any guidance from China, he went ahead and prepared programs. "No Russian music, I know, and no baroque or early music, and no romance," said the maestro. "I will play one American composition in each program."

July 20, 1973
From: Department of State, Washington, DC
To: U.S. Liaison Office, Peking

The time has passed in Eugene Ormandy's summer rehearsal schedules where he is willing to consider changes in concert programs for the PRC [People's Republic of China]. He has therefore decided on three programs. . . . If the Chinese object strongly to any work, he will drop it.

Tenny: Ormandy had heard about a new Chinese composition called the *Yellow River Concerto*, and he was willing to play this with a young Chinese pianist, whose name he had heard from the Europeans.

Eugene Ormandy: Mr. [John] Pritchard of the London Philharmonic and Mr. [Claudio] Abbado of the Vienna Philharmonic, they were in China before us. They both played the concerto with the same wonderful Chinese pianist. Brilliant. His name is Yin Chengzong, about thirty-two, a warm, sweet man, studied in Russia, won a prize in Russia. He played the concerto for them, so I asked him to play with us.

July 20, 1973
From: Department of State, Washington, DC
To: U.S. Liaison Office, Peking

Ormandy is willing to play *Yellow River Concerto* as many times as PRC wishes, but he asks early confirmation that pianist Yin Chengzong will be available to rehearse and perform with the orchestra in China, beginning with his requested rehearsal September 14. The offer to Yin to rehearse and perform with the orchestra

Concerto by Committee

The *Yellow River Concerto* is frequently disparaged by classical-music aficionados as revolutionary schmaltz, but it was—and is—beloved by the Chinese nation. The concerto is more like a national folk song than a monumental work of music. During the Cultural Revolution, Yin Chengzong, a renowned pianist who was a favorite of Mao Zedong's fourth wife, Jiang Qing, led a committee of four that created the concerto, primarily based on a cantata by the composer Xian Xinghai. This was a time when all decisions, even creative ones, had to be inclusive and shaped by committees "of the masses."

In 1969, Yin and his band of composers were dispatched by Madame Mao to remote rural towns along the Yellow River to seek inspiration. They lived among village families and followed boatmen working on the river. Over three months, the team wrote the concerto, which made its debut in 1970. Under the strict controls around music during the Cultural Revolution, Yin and his fellow musicians felt a need to come up with a composition for the piano with a political purpose. The concerto is an homage to the Yellow River, a waterway as embedded in Chinese identity as the Mississippi River is in America. With themes from the cantata by Xian, the concerto echoes such Communist anthems as "The East Is Red" and "The Internationale." "We wanted to create something that people would understand immediately," Yin told the *Philadelphia Inquirer* in 2008, "and all Chinese people love it."

in Saratoga, New York[,] in late August still stands, although early confirmation would be needed if Yin is to be received at Saratoga. The U.S. trip is not a prerequisite for Yin's performance with the orchestra in China, but he will be welcomed if he can make the trip.

Platt: The Chinese did object to certain pieces in the program. They rejected Richard Strauss's "Don Juan" and Claude Debussy's "Afternoon of a Faun" as prurient and decadent. They came back suggesting any piece by Mozart or Schubert, both of whom were considered politically neutral. We had to negotiate every program.

Tenny: Two weeks before the departure date, the orchestra was in Saratoga Springs. I called Sokoloff to tell him we had one answer: "Don't play 'Don Juan.'"

Ormandy: During the last rehearsal in Saratoga, which was really a rehearsal for China, I was rehearsing one work, Richard Strauss's "Don Juan." All of a sudden, I see my assistant

Pianist and composer Yin Chengzong in Shanghai during the 1973 tour. Yin was not permitted to leave China to perform with the Philadelphia Orchestra during its summer residency in Saratoga Springs, New York. The scramble to find a replacement led to a young graduate of the Juilliard School, Daniel Epstein. (Photo by Edward Viner.)

William Smith open the door and ease his way toward me. He knows I don't like to be disturbed when I'm rehearsing. So I kept on rehearsing. He stops and says, "Maestro, I hate to do this to you, but management is on the phone with the Washington liaison office. They just had a call from Peking. They don't want 'Don Juan,' so don't rehearse it." So, we didn't play "Don Juan." I stopped rehearsing it. These are things you learn.

July 25, 1973
From: U.S. Liaison Office, Peking
To: Department of State, Washington, DC

Concerning Ormandy's invitation to pianist Yin Chengzong to come to the United States to perform with the orchestra, Lin [Ping, the Ministry of Foreign Affairs Director for America and Oceania Affairs] said the invitation has been conveyed, but it was his understanding there was virtually no chance of his being able to accept.

Davyd Booth: Unfortunately, they wouldn't let the Chinese pianist out of the country, so we played the *Yellow River Concerto* with a guy by the name of Daniel Epstein.

Daniel Epstein, concert pianist: Ormandy needed someone in a hurry who knew the piece to replace Yin. By coincidence, a friend of mine from high school named Harriet Brickman worked in the publicity office at the Saratoga Music Festival and told the orchestra that I was a pianist with the *Yellow River Concerto* piano score.

Ormandy: I had the music sent to me from China, but it was only the conductor's score. Before the last concert in Saratoga, I found a young American, a New York–born pianist, who knew the *Yellow River Concerto*. The head of the Chinese delegation in the liaison office at the United Nations had given him the score, and he had memorized it.

Epstein: Actually, I hadn't seriously learned the piece. It was literally nine days before the orchestra was set to perform the *Yellow River Concerto* that I got a call from Mr. Ormandy's secretary. She said, "We understand you can play the *Yellow River Concerto*. Would you be available on August 25?" And I said, "Sure." I was flipping out. Right then, I had to drive to his summer home in Tanglewood to audition for him.

Ormandy: It didn't take more than two minutes for me to decide to engage him.

Epstein: I drove home as fast as possible, and I ran to the piano and started practicing. Two hours later, we got a call from Japan that my mother-in-law had died. The next day, I was on a plane for Tokyo. I brought the score and spent the entire flight fingering the music, mostly trying to get it in my head. Forty-eight hours later, I turned around and returned to New York.

Platt: The *Yellow River Concerto* basically was a big piece of program music about the grandeur of the Yellow River. It was written by a committee of party faithful, including Yin, and based on a well-known cantata.

Pianist Epstein with Eugene Ormandy at the Saratoga Performing Arts Center in Saratoga Springs, New York, where Epstein was a late replacement as the soloist for the *Yellow River Concerto*. Long before members of the Philadelphia Orchestra knew that they were going to China, Epstein had obtained a score of the concerto from the Chinese mission at the United Nations. (Courtesy of Daniel Epstein.)

Larry Grika: It was a nice tune, a pleasant tune. In our declaration of great music, it was not. But it reflected something of their heritage, their river, just like Beethoven wrote the *Pastoral* Symphony about his area in Europe.

Epstein: On the morning of the concert, we did a run-through—no rehearsal, just a run-through. The press of the world was there. All the news services, and CBS and NBC. I was interviewed for the *Today Show.* Before we walked on stage, Ormandy said, "Are you nervous?" I said, "I'm not nervous at all." I really wasn't. When you're in your twenties, you think you're invincible.

Ormandy: He played the concerto with us for the first time in the United States. It was a fantastic success. It sounds a little Russian, some of it. It's very effective, but don't ask Mr. [Paul] Hume [of the *Washington Post*] what he thinks of it. He heard it in Saratoga, and he called it something else.

> August 27, 1973
> From: Department of State, Washington, DC
> To: U.S. Liaison Office, Peking
>
> Music critic Paul Hume, in *Washington Post* of August 27, called concerto "schmaltz," "kitsch," "schlock," termed the last movement "sheer, unmitigated bilge," and concluded that a committee cannot write a concerto, but he said the Philadelphia Orchestra's performance brought down the house, and commented that if the concerto were recorded, it would probably become a "runaway best-seller."

Yin Chengzong: I get used to it. Critics see it as light music. At that time, you could not do anything by yourself; it had to be by committee. I never thought this concerto would be a great concerto.

5 | SEPTEMBER 10

Pioneers

With the Philadelphia Police and Firemen's Band playing "Everything's Coming Up Roses" on the tarmac at the Philadelphia International Airport, 130 passengers boarded a special 707 Pan Am charter, renamed "Philadelphia Orchestra." The entourage traveled with 104 cases of instruments, luggage, and equipment. The Chinese hosts held firm on limiting the number of guests, even though some high-powered orchestra benefactors, dangling the offer of tour funding, tried mightily, but unsuccessfully, to get an invitation. Leaving Philadelphia at noon, the group stopped in San Francisco for refueling before continuing on to Honolulu for a one-night layover. The seventy-three-year-old Ormandy was already in Hawaii, having arrived four days earlier to begin acclimating himself to a different time zone. China would be twelve hours ahead of the East Coast.

James Barnes, stagehand: My father, Edward Barnes, joined the orchestra in 1956 as stage manager. It was his job to make sure all the instruments got safely from Philadelphia to China. I was sixteen years old at the time, and I remember when we sent him off what a big deal it was. All I knew about Asia was the Vietnam War that was going on. China was a closed country. My father had been on many tours before, but this was something special.

Eugene Ormandy: We were limited to 130, and the orchestra alone is 105 without me. You can imagine, we didn't have much room for anyone else.

Edward Viner, tour physician: I was thrilled to go. It was my first time traveling with the orchestra. I asked, "How about my wife?" They said, "She can go, but we can't say anything about it." So many people wanted to go with us but had to be turned down.

At the Philadelphia International Airport, musicians climb aboard a Pan Am charter as hundreds cheer them, including family, friends, and such officials as Mayor Frank Rizzo and Tsien Ta-yung, the highest-ranking Chinese official in Washington, DC. Declared Tsien, "This is indeed a cause for rejoicing." (Photo by Alan Abel.)

Judith Viner, tour nurse: We had heard that Ambassador Walter Annenberg and Mayor Frank Rizzo wanted to go but couldn't. I was allowed to be on the docket because I was listed as a nurse, and I am. I did help.

Ormandy: My conducting clothes are always packed in the harp case. The ladies who play the harps are very generous, although I suspect they don't like it. The harp is very bulky, you see. It has forty-seven strings. But there is still room enough for my clothes and the harpist's too.

Alan Abel: We knew it was special from the time we got on the plane to go there, and it remained that way the whole time. You felt as though you were pioneers.

Booker Rowe, violin: We didn't know what to expect. And even on the trip over there, things were still unfolding in terms of the schedule and what we were going to be doing. I knew we'd be playing concerts, but we weren't sure when, where, and under what conditions.

Globetrotters

From its start in 1900, the Philadelphia Orchestra gained a reputation as one of the most peripatetic orchestras in the world. In the early years, musicians regularly traveled to nearby cities a few hours away—Reading, Harrisburg, Scranton, Allentown, Trenton, Wilmington, New York, Baltimore, and Washington, DC. The reasons for touring were both lofty and pragmatic. There was the desire to spread the beauty of the music far and wide as cultural ambassadors as well as the practical need to build an audience and sell records.

In 1917, the orchestra made its first 78 r.p.m. sound recording at the Victor Talking Machine Co. of Camden, New Jersey. Much later, the orchestra's label, RCA Victor, underwrote a coast-to-coast tour in 1936, with Leopold Stokowski and his musicians traveling eleven thousand miles by train to perform thirty-three concerts in thirty days. In 1949, the orchestra, now under the baton of Eugene Ormandy, crossed the Atlantic for the first time and entertained war-weary British audiences, with twenty-eight concerts in twenty-seven days. A tour of continental Europe followed in 1955 that included Ormandy and his musicians visiting Finnish composer Jean Sibelius at his country home. Three years later, the orchestra performed in the Soviet Union as well as in the Communist bloc nations of Poland and Romania. "If you want to see the world, join a great orchestra," recalled violinist Larry Grika, who started as a violinist in 1964, just as the touring itinerary would expand its global reach in a major way. Audiences in Central and South America would hear the Philadelphians in 1966, and Japan became the first Asian stop in 1967.

In the twenty-first century, Asia became a more important market. By 2020, the orchestra had traveled to China a total of twelve times, usually including in its itinerary stops in Japan, South Korea, Hong Kong, Malaysia, or Taiwan. Another milestone came in 1999, when the Philadelphians, under the baton of Wolfgang Sawallisch, became the first American orchestra to perform in Vietnam. The role of cultural diplomat is not without risks. The decision in 2018 to travel to Israel was met with opposition, at home and on the road, with pro-Palestinian demonstrations and concert interruptions during the tour. While the orchestra had never faced such disruptions, Israel-born cellist Udi Bar-David told the *Philadelphia Inquirer* that it was not necessarily a bad thing. "Maybe it's okay to accept that it may happen," he said. "We can't always assume we have the luxury of being on an isolated island."

September 4, 1973
From: Department of State, Washington, DC
To: U.S. Liaison Office, Peking

    Orchestra leaves choice of order in which programs presented up to Chinese, but wishes to be informed somewhat in advance (They said before they got on the stage) which program the Chinese want on which evening.

Larry Grika: On our way to China, we were told that they didn't want us to play all seven of the concerts we were scheduled to perform. Instead, they wanted us to see more of their performances, like ballets and orchestras. Ormandy was completely furious with that because he said, "We're coming to China to play, not to look!"

Davyd Booth: I wasn't even supposed to be on this trip. I had been in Philadelphia to go to school since 1968. I came from a small town in West Virginia, and literally this China trip was my start with the Philadelphia Orchestra. My contract was to start after they got back. But a couple of weeks beforehand, I got a call from the personnel manager who said, "Maestro Ormandy would like you to go." It turns out that somebody had retired, and I took his place. It was the first time out of the country for me. In fact, I didn't even have a passport.

Daniel Webster: There were only a few reporters in the group. I covered the orchestra for the *Philadelphia Inquirer*. Then there was Harold Schonberg, the music critic for the *New York Times*, and Kati Marton, a local television reporter for WCAU, and her cameraman. The *Philadelphia Bulletin* sent Sandy Grady, who was a sports columnist.

Kati Marton, former WCAU-TV reporter: I was twenty-three and had joined the station six months earlier. I was deeply resented for getting this plum assignment as the newest and youngest reporter in the Philadelphia press corps. I had come from Washington, DC, and worked for National Public Radio while earning my master's degree in Sino-Soviet studies from George Washington University. I think that's what gave the news director at WCAU the idea to send me. But I knew all the knives in the newsroom were out for me. All those older guys would have killed for this assignment.

John Krell, piccolo, in his journal: All orderly on plane 'til second drink, then sardine congestion in the aisles. Lunch and professional patience of the crew restored order, but the noise of the plane and raised voices created a limbo of unreality as the ship raced the sun through the tunnel in the sky.

Marton: Like Ormandy, I'm Hungarian. I was born in Budapest. But when I got on the plane, everyone told me, "Don't tell Ormandy you're Hungarian. He doesn't like to talk Hungarian. He doesn't like to admit he's Hungarian. It's not a plus. So don't."

Sheila Platt, wife of Nicholas Platt: [Ormandy] was a tiny man with fluffy hair, immaculately pressed gray suit, and great animation. Mrs. [Gretel] Ormandy was a more massive blond Viennese lady, both charming. Ormandy had a bit of a reputation as a diva. It was "My way or the highway." We were told that his wife, Gretel, usually would cook him chicken and steaks in their room, and no other food would pass his lips. She would make it for him. Period, the end.

WCAU-TV reporter Kati Marton interviews musicians on the Pan Am charter. A newcomer to the Philadelphia press corps, she was the only television reporter who traveled with the orchestra. Marton received a Peabody Award for a documentary about the visit, *Overture to Friendship.* (Photo by Alan Abel.)

September 5, 1973
From: Department of State, Washington, DC
To: U.S. Liaison Office, Peking

Ormandy has again stated his strong preference that he and Mrs. Ormandy not attend any social functions before or after performances unless they are major protocol affairs. The Ormandys are more or less prepared for such a reception on the occasion of the orchestra's first and last performances in China. They have been told of the difficulty of predicting when high-ranking PRC personages may decide to appear on short notice and of course will appear whenever there is any

With their shared Hungarian heritage, Conductor Eugene Ormandy and reporter Marton became friends. After the tour, Ormandy sent her a signed photograph: "To Kati, In happy memories of our unforgettable China tour." (Courtesy of Kati Marton.)

real reason to do so[,] but in view of Ormandy's 73 years[,] he and Mrs. Ormandy prefer not to take part in routine social affairs, and this was stressed to us once more by Sokoloff.

Marton: On the plane, when I noticed that his wife had gotten up to use the bathroom, I immediately swept in and took her seat and started speaking to Ormandy in Hungarian. He was all too happy to speak Hungarian. We were both from the same Budapest intelligentsia— Jewish, very musical. My uncle had been a conductor in Budapest. That was the beginning of our beautiful friendship. And at the end of the trip, he gave me a photograph of us on the Great Wall, signed, "In happy memory of our unforgettable China tour."

6 | SEPTEMBER 11

"Not My First Trumpet!"

The overnight stop on Waikiki Beach brought an unexpected rendezvous: the Cleveland Orchestra was making the same layover en route to Australia and New Zealand. The pink stucco Royal Hawaiian Hotel threw a reception for the touring musicians, many of whom knew each other. The next morning, at 11:00 A.M., the Philadelphia Orchestra continued on to Tokyo before heading to Shanghai.

Francis Tenny: As we gathered at the [Honolulu] airport, Douglas Murray of the National Committee on U.S.-China Relations, who was traveling with us as an escort, adviser, interpreter, collected passports in a pillowcase and counted them. One was missing. A search of hotel rooms, baggage, and other sites yielded nothing.

John Krell: Our principal trumpet, Gil Johnson, who had lost his passport, caused a big delay at the airport, which involved special calls to Washington, plus many jokes about the *Flying Dutchman, A Man Without a Country*, etc.

Tenny: It appeared that Johnson could not continue on the flight to China. "No!" said the maestro. "Take anyone else. My first violin. Anyone, but not my first trumpet. Without him, I do not go."

Krell: Boss was definitely not amused.

Philadelphia Orchestra musicians arrive in Honolulu for an overnight layover. By coincidence, the Cleveland Orchestra was also in town and joined the Philadelphians that night at a reception at their hotel, the Royal Hawaiian. (Photo courtesy of the Philadelphia Orchestra Association Archives, used with kind permission.)

Trumpet principal Gil Johnson, seen here with members of the Central Philharmonic in China, nearly missed the trip because of a lost passport. Diplomats made special arrangements for him. (Photo courtesy of the Philadelphia Orchestra Association Archives, used with kind permission.)

Tenny: A series of fast nighttime and daytime phone calls to Washington, Tokyo, [and] Beijing engineered a quick diplomatic solution. Gil Johnson would board the flight to Tokyo without a passport. He would be met during a brief stop at the Tokyo airport by an American embassy employee bearing a newly minted passport for him to sign. Continuing on to Shanghai, our first trumpeter would be met by a Chinese official who would stamp a visa in his passport.

Sandy Grady, columnist for the *Philadelphia Bulletin*: It took officials from three nations to get Johnson into China. They took a Polaroid photo of him at the airport, rushed it to the U.S. State Department, and had a visa wired to Shanghai. "I thought I was going to be a man without a country," said Johnson.

7 | SEPTEMBER 12

Red Carpet Welcome

Just after 3:00 P.M., the Pan Am charter approached the airport in Shanghai in heavy fog and rain. Nicholas Platt, the U.S. foreign service officer stationed in Beijing whose job was to organize tour details and escort Ormandy in China, flew to Shanghai to meet the plane and relay news sure to upset the maestro.

Eugene Ormandy: There was mystery all over the plane. Everybody came to me, and said, "What do you expect?" I said, "I don't know." At one point, one of my colleagues screamed, "I see land!" *China. The mainland.* We were all excited.

Daniel Webster: No one had a hint of what awaited them in China. *Feicheng* (Mandarin for Philadelphia) was coming. The plane came in low over tilled fields and rolled to a small terminal.

Herb Light, violin: This was unknown territory to the pilot. And I'll never forget, there was rather a low ceiling when we came into Shanghai, and they were going back and forth. And afterward, the pilot told us when we finally got in safely, "Never been here before. Just wanted to make sure."

Ormandy: We didn't know what we were going to face until the door opened in Shanghai, where we had to stop first. I was asked to be the first one to go off the plane and my wife to follow me. There was a red carpet out, and on both sides of the carpet, there were a number of people. On the left side was the diplomatic corps; on the right, the musicians of the local

Leading the way, Conductor Eugene Ormandy, followed by his wife, Gretel, arrives at the airport in Beijing on September 12, 1973. He is shaking hands with the conductor of the Central Philharmonic Society, Li Delun.
(Photo courtesy of the Philadelphia Orchestra Association Archives, used with kind permission.)

Classical Music in China

European music was introduced by Jesuit missionaries to the Chinese imperial court in the seventeenth century and used as a tool of religious conversion as well as of diplomacy. Foreign armies also had military bands. In fact, later during the warlord era that began in 1916, some Chinese militarists wanted bands of their own and hired German instructors to organize and train them. By the early twentieth century, classical music could be heard in such urban centers as Shanghai, Beijing, and the Russian-influenced northern city of Harbin. Chinese students returning from study abroad brought home a love of Beethoven and other composers. By the 1920s, the art form was becoming more popular in cosmopolitan centers but still had limited reach.

Authors Sheila Melvin and Jindong Cai write in *Beethoven in China: How the Great Composer Became an Icon in the People's Republic* (Penguin Books, 2015) that Beethoven became a favorite of Chinese intellectuals, celebrated for his perseverance in the face of adversity. After the rise of the People's Republic of China in 1949, Communist leaders debated whether classical music was bourgeois and should be eliminated or whether it could be adopted to serve workers, peasants, and soldiers. Over the course of the 1950s, given the strong Soviet influence over China at the time, those who believed that Western symphonic music could serve the people held an edge in ongoing political debates. In 1959, to celebrate the tenth anniversary of the founding of the People's Republic, musicians with the Central Philharmonic Society performed Beethoven's Ninth Symphony for the first time with an all-Chinese orchestra and chorus in Chinese. With the start of the Cultural Revolution in 1966, however, the situation abruptly changed, with classical musicians and the music that they played denounced as examples of old ways that had to be destroyed.

symphony orchestra, all applauding us. They were just as warm and wonderful as could be. We only spent an hour and half at the airport until they [put] gasoline into our plane.

Nicholas Platt: I had left for Shanghai to meet the orchestra's plane and fly with them to Beijing. I had hoped to be able to get together with the Ministry of Culture officials handling the visit from the Chinese side. But I was held at arm's length until twenty-five minutes before the orchestra landed. That was when Mr. Situ [Huacheng], the glum but competent concertmaster of the Central Philharmonic Society, entered the VIP lounge where I was waiting. He sat down and told me with deep apologies that certain revisions in the programs would be required. The biggest issue was performing Beethoven's Sixth Symphony. It had been discussed throughout the negotiations leading up to Ormandy's arrival. The Chinese desire to include it—and Ormandy's negative attitude about it—were known but left unresolved until now. I dreaded raising it with an exhausted eminence I had never met.

Sheila Platt: Because the rules kept being changed, Nick had to give Ormandy bad or complicated news every step of the way. And Ormandy arrived sort of with his lip stuck out about all the things he wasn't going to do.

Nicholas Platt: The leadership now wanted concerts that packaged Beethoven's Sixth, an American composition, and the *Yellow River Concerto*. I told Situ I would do my best to work the changes but feared the consequences of confronting Ormandy with major issues after more than twenty hours of grueling travel.

John Krell: The airport was almost deserted and had an eerie frontier atmosphere. Mao caps and buttons began to appear, and my friend bought me a Chinese beer. Waitress refused our proffered token of two American coins even though my friend went through an elaborate charade to equate Lincoln and Washington to Chairman Mao.

Nicholas Platt: We got on the plane for Beijing. The issue of Beethoven's Sixth was crucial to the success of the visit. Confronting difficult topics is what diplomats are paid for. So, I sat down next to Ormandy and plunged in. I told him, "Maestro, we have a request from the top levels of government to play Beethoven's Sixth Symphony." And he looked at me and he said, "You know I hate Beethoven's Sixth. I didn't bring the scores. I don't want to play it."

After a brief layover in Shanghai to refuel and pick up a Chinese crew to help navigate the flight to Beijing, Ormandy and his musicians are greeted on the tarmac at the Capital Airport by Chinese musicians. (Photo courtesy of the Philadelphia Orchestra Association Archives, used with kind permission.)

Light: Ormandy being Ormandy, nobody told *him* what to play, and he was furious.

Nicholas Platt: I said, "Let me try to explain to you why they think Beethoven's Sixth is so important." And I just started making things up.

Light: Ormandy did not hate the Sixth. But I think Ormandy felt that the Sixth Symphony was not showing off the orchestra to his liking. That's the only reason he rebelled against it.

Nicholas Platt: I told him, first of all, the Chinese loved program music, music that represents scenes. Second of all, this is a government that came to power on the backs of a peasant revolution, and pastoral symphonies are all about peasants and farming life. And in the fourth movement, a big storm comes up, and, of course, they think that's the revolution. Then, there is a very peaceful, quiet ending, which they regard as the triumph of the Communist Party. Ormandy looks at me, and he rolls his eyes.

Light: I think he was convinced by Nick Platt that Chinese-American relations were at stake here unless he decided to give in.

Nicholas Platt: Ormandy sighed and said, "If that's what they want, that's what they shall have. I am in Rome and will do as the Romans. I will forget my own rules." I almost collapsed with relief. I told Sokoloff about our conversation and advised him to keep Ormandy's willingness to play the Sixth in his back pocket during the protracted negotiations that were bound to follow.

Krell: Two more hours of flying took us to Peking, where a corridor of applauding officials, augmented by members of the Central Philharmonic Society, greeted us. Too dazed by travel to respond effectively, we settled into our assigned buses and traveled along a dimly lit, tree-lined boulevard into the city, with the constant horns of cars alerting the nocturnal bicyclists.

Ormandy: On the way to town, the musical head of the friendship committee sat with me, and the first question was, "Don't you like the Sixth Symphony of Beethoven?"
I said, "Oh yes, very much."
"Well why didn't you program it?"
This was a very strange question because I had sent a number of programs, and I [had] received no answer.
I said, "Why didn't you ask for it?"
We went on with other things.
This was a thirty-kilometer trip, very slow. The whole orchestra was behind us in cars and buses.
As we arrived in our hotel in Peking, he said to me, "Do you like *Pastoral* Symphony?"

Conductor Ormandy with Li Delun, the Moscow-trained conductor of the Central Philharmonic Society and Ormandy's escort over the course of the tour. Diplomat Nicholas Platt describes Li as an "expansive politico-musician whose personality was cut from much the same cloth as Ormandy's—obviously, the Chinese version of a maestro." (Photo courtesy of the Philadelphia Orchestra Association Archives, used with kind permission.)

I said, "Yes, I told you an hour ago."

He said, "But would you play it?"

I said, "We can play it. But we don't have the music."

He said, "Don't worry, we have it."

I said, "But your bowings and your phrasings are so different from my bowing and my phrasing. I make them all myself."

He said, "That's all right. We'll get it for you."

8 | SEPTEMBER 13

Tug of War

It was after midnight when the orchestra entourage arrived at the Qianmen Hotel in central Beijing, not far from the Temple of Heaven and the Forbidden City. While musicians settled into their rooms, orchestra management, accompanied by diplomats Francis Tenny and Nicholas Platt, sat down to negotiate the final details with Chinese representatives.

Francis Tenny: For the next four hours of the early morning, we asked our questions. Where were the concerts to be? What cities, what hours, what programs? When and what would the musicians eat? They had to eat after the concerts, so what time? What kind of menus, and what about bus pickup time? And above all, what programs for what dates? . . . Boris Sokoloff clearly knew of Ormandy's dislike for the Sixth, and he was doing his best to block the request.

Louis Hood, public relations director of the Philadelphia Orchestra: Formalities were observed over orange soda and tea. It was amazing to learn that concerts could start at the orchestra's convenience and that dates could be easily altered and augmented at this late date—and hour.

Tenny: After some fifteen minutes, [a cultural attaché named Mr. Liu] said, "We'd like for you to play Beethoven's Sixth Symphony."

"Oh," Sokoloff said. "If you had asked us earlier, we would have been delighted to prepare and play the Sixth. But Maestro doesn't play it too often. He hasn't played it in some years, and we don't have the music with us."

Again, after some time, Mr. Liu reverted to: "What about Beethoven's Sixth?"

"We don't have the music, as I told you, so it is out of the question," Sokoloff said. He did, however, send someone to awaken the music librarian and ask him to join us. When the librarian arrived, Sokoloff asked him whether he had brought the music for Beethoven's Sixth. "No," the librarian answered in surprise. "You didn't tell me to, and you know the maestro hasn't played it in years."

The discussion reverted to bus times, menus, and places of concerts. Another twenty minutes and Mr. Liu repeated, "What about Beethoven's Sixth?"

"I'm sorry, but it's out of the question. We don't have the scores," Sokoloff repeated.

"But," said Mr. Liu, "we will loan you the scores. Our orchestras have them."

"Thank you," said Sokoloff, "but we have a large orchestra, and we would need at least 115 sets of parts."

"That's all right," said Mr. Liu. "We have orchestras all over China, and we will have the scores flown in for you tomorrow."

The group recessed at about 4:00 A.M. with Mr. Liu's repeated request, "We want Beethoven's Sixth."

Our group recessed for four hours and met again to call on the maestro and Mrs. Ormandy as they were eating breakfast in their suite. Sokoloff told him about the repeated requests for Beethoven's Sixth. The maestro looked at the three of us and said, "So what do I do?"

"Play the Sixth!" we said in unison.

Nicholas Platt: That was one crisis averted. The officials who worked for Madame Mao were scared to death of her. And I knew that if we could fix this one thing, then everything would fall in place.

Tenny: No one ever told us who had ordered Beethoven's Sixth. We did surmise that it was Madame Mao herself. She had, after all, been a film actress in Shanghai before the war, and she must have seen the Disney film *Fantasia*, set to the music of Beethoven's Sixth. Chinese officials, however, explained that the Sixth was desired because it reflected the rural farm life dear to the ideals of the Chinese Revolution.

Facing page: Tiananmen, the Gate of Heavenly Peace. On their first full day in Beijing, musicians awoke to a city unlike any other. What struck most of them was how bicycles were the only way to get around. (Photo by Edward Viner.)

Madame Mao's Grip

The debate over which Beethoven symphony to perform revealed the long reach of Chairman Mao's fourth wife, Jiang Qing. When the orchestra arrived in China, the country was still in the throes of the disruptive Cultural Revolution that began in 1966. Mao believed that the revolution that he started in 1949 was stagnating, and he was paranoid about political rivals trying to usurp his power. He launched the Cultural Revolution to "destroy the old to build the new" and, for the first two years, unleashed young Red Guards to tear down traditional society. Mao preached that to build a new China, the country had to demolish the "four olds"—old customs, old habits, old culture, and old thinking. Music and art had to serve peasants, workers, and soldiers, not just the intellectual elite and bourgeoisie. From the wreckage of old society, he wanted to build new revolutionary Chinese art and culture, and he put his wife, a former film actress, in charge. She worked with three close associates from Shanghai, who were later disparaged after Mao's death in 1976 as the notorious Gang of Four.

During the Cultural Revolution, orchestras were banned from performing works by Western composers. Instead of Beethoven or Mozart, only eight Chinese-composed "model" productions with revolutionary themes, from operas to symphonic music and ballets, were allowed. (The number had increased to eighteen by the latter part of the Cultural Revolution.) The early years of the Cultural Revolution were so chaotic and damaging that Mao eventually had to rein in the violence, restoring order and urging urban youth to work on communes to "learn from peasants." Millions of young people took up the call to toil in the fields. But he did not rein in his wife, who continued to use the arts and culture in the name of revolution. The 1973 visit by the Philadelphians gave American diplomats a rare opportunity to see Madame Mao in action. They analyzed her every move, including her obsession with Beethoven's Sixth Symphony, to divine what was happening behind the scenes with the Communist leadership.

A street in central Beijing.
(Photo by Alan Abel.)

On their first morning in Beijing, the Philadelphians ventured into the streets around the Qianmen Hotel.

Sandy Grady: Nostalgic sound of horse carts in the street. Bikes everywhere, wheeling down a wide avenue. Fleets of birds. Car horns—the Chinese make the Schuylkill Expressway sound like a chapel. Young pioneers in red bandannas marching in a schoolyard. Curious stares everywhere. Stop to shoot a picture, a mob gathers. We're instant freaks—except for the orchestra, there are only forty Americans in China.

John Krell: The morning flood of bicycles was in force (with a population of 4 million, there are 1½ million cycles) and all, by some form of consensus, pedaled *moderato.*

Julia Janson, violin: Our hotel rooms were very plain, very stark. We called it "Early YMCA." There were no decorations and no locks on the doors, which was unusual.

Left, top: Beijing residents marveling at a Polaroid photograph. Wherever they went, the Philadelphians attracted crowds, and many of the musicians carried Polaroid cameras with them. (Photo courtesy of the Philadelphia Orchestra Association Archives, used with kind permission.)

Left, bottom: Violinist Booker Rowe outside the Qianmen Hotel in central Beijing. (Photo by Alan Abel.)

Larry Grika: In your room, if you hung up your shirt on a doorknob, it was pressed clean a few hours later. One guy left his old shoes in the wastebasket. He wanted to throw them away. The shoes were delivered back to him when we were leaving at the airport.

Booker Rowe: On the plane, we were told that we should not walk around in groups of more than three or less than two. They didn't want us to draw attention. But that first morning, I needed to get out by myself. I wandered down an alley and came across a little courtyard. All of a sudden, I heard cheering. All these children were clapping and looking at me. We had also been told that at concerts, it's customary for the musicians to applaud back to the audience, thanking them for coming. So that's what I did. When the children applauded me, I applauded back to them.

Margarita Csonka Montanaro: I was three months pregnant at the time. I didn't make a big deal about it. There were only seven women in the orchestra, and you didn't want to act weak. Before we went, the orchestra management told us women that we should all wear pants in China and not to wear skirts. Well, I always wore skirts. I went for a walk with my husband [clarinetist Donald Montanaro], and it was one of those streets filled with people, tons of people. While I was walking, a semicircle formed around me, all these

Right, top: WCAU's Kati Marton conducts a man-on-the-street interview in Beijing. Marton made a point of swapping her short skirt for a Mao suit to be less conspicuous. (Photo courtesy of the Philadelphia Orchestra Association Archives, used with kind permission.)

Right, bottom: A parking lot of identical Flying Pigeon bicycles. (Photo courtesy of the Philadelphia Orchestra Association Archives, used with kind permission.)

people staring at me and my legs. Everybody looked alike. They wore either gray or dark blue suits, no colors.

Kati Marton: I was trying to film on Tiananmen Square, which is a mammoth-size square. In those days, I was wearing a miniskirt, as we all were. Literally, bicycle traffic came to a halt. They piled up behind me. They hadn't seen a girl's legs in years. I had to go into the People's Department Store and buy a baggy Mao suit so I could proceed. I didn't do any on-camera appearances in that unflattering outfit, but it did enable me to get around. It was my incognito uniform—as if I could fool anyone!

Grady: I tried some Chinese-in-the-street interviews. Ten people were asked what they knew about "the Watergate affair in the United States." Polite stares. Nice, big smiles. Some giggling. It was like stopping ten guys on Broad Street and asking them to explain the infield fly rule. It was also comforting—a big chunk of the world isn't in a swivet over [G. Gordon] Liddy and [H. R.] Haldeman and Martha [Mitchell]'s latest telephone jeremiad. "Ah, Watergate—we hope your fine president is not arrested," said one passerby, smiling like a Republican ward leader.

Krell: At 2:30 P.M., a convoy of buses took us to a concert by folk artists and the Central Philharmonic Society at a nearby hall. The

A chorus welcomes the Philadelphia Orchestra with a rendition of "America the Beautiful." Veteran China-watchers noted that the women were wearing traditional-style tops instead of unisex Mao suits.
(Photo by Edward Viner.)

concert opened with excellent chorus (pinched, piercing quality to the female voices) singing "America the Beautiful" (last chorus in astonishingly good English), followed by spirited revolutionary songs, all done with subtle dynamics and style.

Sheila Platt: The hall, where the Philadelphia Orchestra would also play, was rather small, but quite brilliant. The concert was opened by a mixed chorus, the ladies, all middle-aged, wearing white satin *qipao* jackets [a type of traditional fitted dress or top] and mid-calf-length pale blue tulle skirts and sparkles. They very beautifully sang "America the Beautiful," seriously like a hymn. We were all moved.

Hood: It was interesting to note that the line "God shed His grace on thee" came out loud and clear.

Krell: After the intermission were more selections on native instruments, including a remarkable battle depiction (*Ambushes on All Sides*) on a pipa (elaborate lute) with quite extraordinary technique. Surprisingly, all the native instruments in the faster movements sound like Hungarian rhapsodies—Hungarians must have stolen that too—but it does imply a propulsive drive common to all folk-dance music. Concert closed with a cantata (accompanied by the Philharmonic) based on poems of Chairman Mao.

––––––––––

The day closed with a welcome banquet at the Peking Hotel, a block from the Forbidden City.

Xinhua News Agency: The Philadelphia Orchestra is the first cultural group from the U.S.A. to visit the People's Republic of China. Both Chinese and American artists were glad to have this opportunity to meet in Peking. They repeatedly clinked glasses at the banquet to the constant growth of the friendship between the people of the two countries.

Sheila Platt: We had, at table 4, the Chinese and American assistant conductors, horn players, and Nicky's opposite number from the American Department of the Foreign Office. The meal was delicious and both nationalities charming, I thought. We interpreted throughout, and also to the Chinese. One man told me he sang "America the Beautiful" very often before the liberation, as it was in the book of 101 songs in his school in Shanghai, a church school. They all joked about their May 7 Cadre School [labor camps started during the Cultural Revolution that combined farm work with the study of Mao's writing in order to "reeducate" intellectuals and cadres] where they go and *lao dung* [labor] for six months at a time. It was a fruit farm, and there were jokes about musicians delicately clipping the twigs so as not to hurt their hands. Also, said the assistant conductor, they got to eat a lot of fruit.

Krell: Gil Johnson, Sam Krauss, and I were seated with five Chinese—an interpreter, a film producer, a trombone and a viola player from the Central Philharmonic, and a personable young girl director of *Voice of Peking Radio*. All most convivial and gracious. *Maotai* liquor (pungent taste), a good dry red wine, and beer all promptly replenished as consumed.

Conductor Eugene Ormandy makes a toast at the first of
many banquets in honor of the musicians. (Photo courtesy of the
Philadelphia Orchestra Association Archives, used with kind permission.)

Sheila Platt: My favorite moment was an American saying to a Chinese who was helping him get another dish, "*Poco pianissimo* [a little softer]," whereupon the whole table burst into musical Italian. Mr. Ormandy's toast was charming and warm, and the evening was a success in spite of the Americans' jet lag.

Grady: At one table, Mr. Situ Huacheng, the concertmaster [of the Central Philharmonic], asked, "Tell me seriously, how does our orchestra sound to you?"

"Fine," said Norman Carol, the Philadelphia concertmaster, "but you could be more fluid with the bow, more flowing with the wrist, like this. . . ."

It may have been the first demonstration of how to play a violin using chopsticks.

Krell: I subsequently learned that the concertmaster had memorized all the names of the Philadelphia Orchestra men and even the make of their instruments.

> September 15, 1973
> From: U.S. Liaison Office, Peking
> To: Secretary of State, Washington, DC
>
> Chinese clearly delighted with the orchestra's accommodating attitude. At notably cordial welcoming banquet at Peking Hotel [on] Sept. 13, Friendship Association Vice President Lin Lin remembered in his toast that Ormandy had conducted a benefit concert in 1940 organized by Norman Bethune for China relief. (Ormandy has vague recollection of concert.) Fact that Chinese have chosen to take public note of this event seems further mark of their intent to make Philadelphia Orchestra Tour a success.

9 | SEPTEMBER 14

Opening Night

The Philadelphia Orchestra only had one rehearsal during its ten-day tour, and, much to Ormandy's dismay, it would be open to observers, mostly Chinese musicians. He groused to Daniel Webster of the *Inquirer*, "I don't rehearse for an audience. Even musicians would not know what I am doing by stopping and starting and jumping around in the scores." But Ormandy relented and allowed a small audience at the Hall of Chinese Nationalities. This also was the only chance the orchestra had to rehearse Beethoven's Sixth as well as the *Yellow River Concerto* with guest soloist Yin Chengzong.

Nicholas Platt: That morning, we did get the scores for Beethoven's Sixth. They got seventy scores from Shanghai and sixty scores from Beijing. All the bowing marks and dynamics were marked up in different ways, but the orchestra didn't care. They knew that symphony cold.

Larry Grika: You're talking about the Philadelphia Orchestra. You're talking about Beethoven. How many times have we played Beethoven's Sixth? How many times have we played *any* of the Beethoven symphonies? It wouldn't have mattered if some pages were missing.

Eugene Ormandy: The orchestration was entirely different from ours. Naturally, every orchestra plays differently, bowing wise, not interpretively. I gave a pass to my musicians. I said, "My dear friends, we have to play this. We'll just rehearse it and just play it."

Typical of musicians, a colleague complained, "My bowings are so different from his in front!"

I said, "Forget it. Play free bowing like we did in the past."

The technique of free bowing was popularized by Ormandy's predecessor, Leopold Stokowski, who allowed each string player to determine individually how to play a set of notes.

Ormandy: Stokowski always believed in free bowing. I said, "Play like Stokowski." So, that settled that. No more questions.

Herb Light: Every score was individually handwritten. We had one rehearsal with it. Of course, the orchestra knew the symphony backward. The score was full of mistakes, and we would be playing along and—*whoops, wrong note.* And it was sort of hilarious because once you knew that the note was wrong, you didn't play it.

Zhang Dihe, Central Philharmonic oboist: The musicians were onstage for the rehearsal. I sat on the second floor of the concert hall, close to the stage. I could hear the practicing of the oboe principal, John de Lancie. When he made his first sound, I was shocked. I had been playing the oboe for more than twenty years. I had never heard such a sound from an oboe. It filled the whole theater. It had a different beauty—relaxed, wide and soft, with wide amplitude. I was really impressed.

After a run-through of the *Pastoral* Symphony, Ormandy and the musicians turned to the *Yellow River Concerto.*

Nicholas Platt: Yin Chengzong was the most famous pianist in the People's Republic in the 1970s, a roly-poly protégé of Madame Mao's who made his name performing the *Yellow River Concerto.*

John Krell: Boss was in a complete dither. Young, plump soloist played the *Yellow River Concerto* (written by a committee) in a very rhapsodic style, which upsets the boss, who was divided between impressing the [rehearsal] audience of Chinese orchestra musicians and trying to make semblance of order out of an otherwise chaotic situation. His temper surfaced but was contained, and, for the first time, he admitted to being in a circumstance where he had no control.

Above: Conductor Ormandy leads his orchestra through Beethoven's Sixth Symphony with borrowed scores. Musicians saw a different maestro that day: one who capitulated to the circumstances. He told the string section to "play like Stokowski" with free bowing because the scores lacked their usual bowing notations.
(Photo courtesy of the Philadelphia Orchestra Association Archives, used with kind permission.)

Facing page: At the one and only rehearsal during the tour, Conductor Eugene Ormandy and pianist Yin Chengzong *(right)* review the score of the *Yellow River Concerto* with an unidentified translator.
(Photo courtesy of the Philadelphia Orchestra Association Archives, used with kind permission.)

A Chinese musician playing the pipa joins the Philadelphia Orchestra for a run-through of the *Yellow River Concerto*. (Photo courtesy of the Philadelphia Orchestra Association Archives, used with kind permission.)

Nicholas Platt: Ormandy was strangely frustrated. During rehearsal, Yin never looked at him and didn't respond to any of his directions. There was sort of a disconnect there, and Ormandy was frustrated by it. He and Yin got along extremely well. I mean, they were both musicians, and they obviously both were *good* musicians. But Ormandy was critical of Yin for not watching and not being completely in rhythm.

Ormandy: The score that I received from China through the liaison office in Washington was beautifully bound, and it says, "Composed by a Committee." And that's all it says. So, when I got there, I asked Mr. Yin, "What sort of committee is this? In our country, only one person composes."

He said originally this was a cantata for chorus and orchestra. The composer [Xian Xinghai] had composed it during the war against Japan, and he [had] died in that war.

Yin said to me, "I rewrote it for the piano to fit my technique."

It's full of cadenzas. Jumps up and down all the time. I said to him, "Who else composed it?"

And he turned to Mr. Li [Delun, conductor of the Central Philharmonic]—they are very close friends—and said, "Well, he helped me, and he orchestrated it. That's the committee."

Louis Hood: The opening concert on Friday, September 14, attracted a capacity crowd to the Hall of the Chinese Nationalities. Chinese custom is not to play national anthems to open a program, so the music began with Mozart's *Haffner* Symphony, followed by Roy Harris's Symphony no. 3 [and] Brahms's Symphony no. 1.

Emilio Gravagno: That program represented the stretch of the orchestra— being able to play very classical music and being able to play the Roy Harris piece, which was much more contemporary sounding. It did show the length and breadth of the orchestra's repertoire.

Nicholas Platt: All of the concerts had audiences that had been handpicked. They didn't want any incidents.

Daniel Webster: The press people had a handler from the foreign ministry, Miss Wu Xiliang. Everything was so controlled. We were not able to speak to people, so it was hard to know who the people in the audience were.

Sheila Platt: There was a real buzz of excitement in the hall, unlike any other performance I'd gone to there. There was a block of empty seats behind us, probably ambassadors who neither showed nor allocated their tickets. The musicians barely fit on the stage and were in white tie and tails, looking nervous.

Nicholas Platt: The audience reaction to the first Mozart piece was quite subdued.

Renard Edwards, viola: It was a huge hall and absolutely silent. I think they were waiting for the senior political folks to put their hands together before the rest of them did.

Before the first concert of the tour, Conductor Ormandy confers with soloist Yin Chengzong, the pianist who led a committee that wrote the *Yellow River Concerto*. (Photo courtesy of the Philadelphia Orchestra Association Archives, used with kind permission.)

Nicholas Platt: Ormandy was upset, and I was called backstage during the intermission, and I found him in a snit. He was standing there and jumping up and down, and his wife, Gretel, was fanning him with a big towel. He was saying, "I've never had such a bad reaction! These people hate this music."

And I said, "Maestro, this is China, and this is the Cultural Revolution. This is the first American orchestra they've heard. It's very reserved, but by my sights, it's very enthusiastic. There's tremendous curiosity about what you are doing here, and I think it's a very positive reaction."

Grika: There was a French reporter backstage, and after we played one of the big works, we heard sort of a temperate, quiet applause, and he said, "They went wild!"

"That's wild?" I said.

"That's wild, for them, that's wild, yes!"

Sheila Platt: Ormandy, perspiring (our delicious September cool felt hot to them), gave a press conference in his dressing room, and we all went back to the hotel. I found myself surrounded for a time by disgruntled musicians, feeling the applause [was] thin and wondering why on Earth they had come. I explained about the "dangers" of things foreign [given the purging of everything bourgeois during the Cultural Revolution] and that the audience seemed unusually warm to me.

Krell: Inside joke: Baby cries on our [hotel] floor. Roommate says, "That's no baby, that's the boss reading last night's reviews."

Robert de Pasquale, violin: Before joining the Philadelphia Orchestra, I was with the New York Philharmonic. In 1959, Lenny Bernstein was the conductor, and we went to the Soviet Union. When we played in Moscow, they practically jumped out of their skin. Shostakovich's Fifth Symphony was such a hit. They're all kissing and hugging Lenny. Up in the balcony, they're clapping, clapping, clapping. They wouldn't let us go. When we walked out of the concert hall, they were still applauding. China, the exact opposite. That first concert in China, they were really very reserved with applause. You never knew if they liked it or not. But as they got used to us, things got warmer.

Turned Tables

Another surprise for Eugene Ormandy: The Central Philharmonic wanted the maestro to conduct them in a rehearsal. Because of the Cultural Revolution—and the banning of performances of Western music by Chinese orchestras—the conductor Li Delun hoped Ormandy would lead his musicians in a private run-through of Beethoven's Fifth Symphony. Not wanting to cause an international incident, Ormandy agreed. The get-together between the two orchestras took place at a compound in the northern part of the city, where members of the Central Philharmonic lived and worked.

Louis Hood: Eugene Ormandy led the way, and the caravan of cars and buses was greeted with waves of applause by several hundred school-age children as it arrived.

John Krell: Their modest and affable conductor, Mr. Li, explained their commune life and working conditions. The large group (orchestra, chorus, folk musicians, composers, [and] theory and administrative staff) lived and worked together with six buildings at their disposal. Meals were eaten together, and they had medical clinics for singers' throats and massage therapy for musicians' fingers.

Francis Tenny: The Chinese orchestra conductor made a speech of welcome: "We are so happy to have you come and to hear you play Beethoven. We have not played Beethoven in years, but since you are here, we would like to show you how we can."

Nicholas Platt: Clearly a second-rate conductor, his leadership and political skills obviously made him the ideal honcho for a cultural organization at this stage in China. He knew a

Hundreds of children applaud as a caravan of buses transporting the orchestra arrives at the rehearsal hall of the Central Philharmonic Society. Philadelphia Orchestra members listened to their Chinese counterparts perform Beethoven's Fifth Symphony—the highlight of the tour for many. (Photo courtesy of the Philadelphia Orchestra Association Archives, used with kind permission.)

great deal about music, had the presence to handle himself well when the national leaders were around, and [had] the managerial ability and sense of humor to run a large communal cultural organization.

Daniel Webster: The orchestra was pitiful. Members held chipped and glued instruments, and they played music that was hand-copied and pasted together from decades before. These musicians had been mining coal and doing field work since 1966, and a few months prior, they were suddenly brought back to reintroduce Western music.

Zhang Dihe: The Cultural Revolution started in 1966, and it had been seven years since we [had] touched a classical symphony piece. Suddenly, we are sitting before Ormandy, one of the greatest conductors in the world.

Cui Zhuping, Central Philharmonic violinist: Young people today do not understand what we experienced. During the Cultural Revolution, Western music was banned; only "model operas" were allowed.

Zhang: The Central Phil used to perform the *Shajiabang* Symphony and *Yellow River Concerto* for piano. They were all composed by groups. We could only perform these revolutionary "model operas," not others.

Liu Qi, Central Philharmonic bassoonist: There was no preparation. We had one rehearsal for this.

Hood: Li Delun conducted his seventy-five-man orchestra in a delicate, contemporary Chinese work titled "Moon Reflected in Two Fountains." He then led a rehearsal of the first movement of Beethoven's Fifth Symphony.

Harold Schonberg, music critic for the *New York Times*: Then came Li's little surprise. He mentioned an article that had appeared in a British magazine after the visit of the London

Bourgeois Targets

In the most violent early years of the Cultural Revolution, classical musicians suffered inordinately. They were representative of the old, foreign culture that had to be eradicated from society. Young Red Guards would target and attack musicians, ransacking their homes, smashing instruments and record albums, and humiliating musicians by placing dunce caps on their heads and derogatory placards around their necks. A violin professor at the Shanghai Conservatory of Music was accused by Red Guards of "dressing like a Westerner" and locked in a closet for nine months. When he was released, Tan Shuzhen was forced to clean 122 toilets a day. A pianist at the conservatory was forced to crawl on the ground and silently submit to Red Guards who poured ink over her head. Li Cuizhen committed suicide, one of seventeen professors at the esteemed school to end their lives, according to authors Sheila Melvin and Jindong Cai. By 1973, when the Philadelphia Orchestra arrived in China, order had returned to society, but there were still strict controls on art and music. The Central Philharmonic was permitted to rehearse Beethoven's Fifth Symphony, but only for a private audience behind closed doors.

After warming up the Central Philharmonic, Conductor Li Delun invites Eugene Ormandy to take over the rehearsal. (Photo courtesy of the Philadelphia Orchestra Association Archives, used with kind permission.)

Philharmonic to China [the previous] March. The author of the article paid tribute to Chinese musicians' playing of Chinese music but went on to say that they had no idea of Western music.

Eugene Ormandy: Mr. Li turned to me and said, "We want to learn, Mr. Ormandy. Will you conduct the second movement?"

Schonberg: It was clear that [Li] was out to prove how wrong the British writer was.

Ormandy: At first, I felt uneasy. What am I doing conducting his orchestra? But I got up. I went, took off my jacket, and conducted the second movement.

Zhang: The flute principal was sitting next to me. His heart was beating very fast. His arm was shaking. I was already very nervous. Mr. Ormandy walked to the stage to conduct the

Li welcomes Ormandy to the podium.
(Photo courtesy of the Philadelphia Orchestra
Association Archives, used with kind permission.)

second movement. I became even more nervous. I missed one or two beats. I was not able to make a sound!

Cui: When we began playing the first movement conducted by Li Delun, we went all out and tried our best. Yet when Ormandy began conducting—*ah*, he had completely brought all the deep emotions. He would give us a gesture, point at us, or just give us a look, and I would take the cue immediately.

Shedding his jacket, Ormandy conducts the Chinese musicians. Chinese and American observers agreed that after just a few minutes under his baton, the Central Philharmonic musicians started to sound markedly better. (Photo courtesy of the Philadelphia Orchestra Association Archives, used with kind permission.)

Zhang: Ormandy was not tall, yet as soon as he was at the podium, his gestures and his eyes could reach every player. That is the mark of a great conductor.

Cui: It almost felt like he was conducting me. He brought me into the music.

Ormandy: They watched everything I said, everything I did. I often say to young conductors, "You don't have to say too much. Just do it in your hands."

Anthony Orlando, percussion: Within a matter of minutes, they actually started to sound like the Philadelphia Orchestra. Ormandy had a chemistry about him that allowed the strings especially to blossom in a way that very few conductors allowed orchestras to do. That was done instinctively by balancing the winds and the brass along with the strings. And so, just through hand motions and the way Mr. Ormandy was moving his hands, he was able to bring the orchestra together in a way that created a sound that was reminiscent of us.

Zhu Gongqi, Central Philharmonic violinist: A famous Chinese author was there when Mr. Ormandy conducted the second movement. She told a newspaper [that] the Central Philharmonic was a completely different orchestra in the second movement under the conducting of Mr. Ormandy. She was right. As a conductor, he inspired us. It's not simply technical, like telling us the correct beat. You could use a metronome to correct a beat, right? We were all very careful to observe and watch and follow his intentions. A good conductor could make an ordinary orchestra play well, and Mr. Ormandy proved that saying.

———

Afterward, the two orchestras exchanged gifts. Ormandy presented Li Delun with new instruments—a trumpet, clarinet, flute, drumheads, and triangles—as well as a stack of Philadelphia Orchestra recordings, books about music, and a collection of scores by American composers. The Chinese conductor presented the Americans with a three-foot brass gong, a large vermilion Chinese drum, a collection of traditional Chinese instruments—bamboo flute, pipa, *sheng*, *erhu*, *suona*—and a score for the *Yellow River Concerto*.

Zhang: Mr. Ormandy also gave each member of the Central Phil a ballpoint pen with the date of the tour in English and Chinese. This was a pretty memorable pen, so I kept it.

Chinese Gifts

In the gift exchange, the musicians of the Central Philharmonic gave their counterparts a collection of Chinese instruments. They included a pipa, a four-stringed instrument; a *sheng*, a mouth-blown reed instrument with vertical pipes; a two-stringed *erhu* played with a bow; and an ancient *suona*, a double-reed horn. Anthony Orlando, a percussionist, said the gong had a very deep tone, but the ringing faded too quickly and could not be used in performances on a regular basis. The gift gong is currently stored in the orchestra's percussion room.

Michael "Mickey" Bookspan *(left)*, the principal percussionist for the Philadelphia Orchestra, and Anthony Orlando accept a gong from their counterparts with the Central Philharmonic Society.
(Photo by Alan Abel.)

Krell: Conductor Li invited a mixing up of Chinese and American musicians, and a great din accumulated as each section went off into corners to explore and demonstrate their respective instruments. I played a bit of Debussy's "Syrinx" (not known here), and a nice man on the bamboo flute imitated it immediately.

Larry Grika: We didn't know what the Cultural Revolution was all about. But we were told by the pianist who played with us in concert that he wasn't allowed to play Chopin in public, he wasn't allowed to play Liszt in public. He said, "Yes, we practice, we learn it." But he was not allowed to perform it.

Nicholas Platt: The Chinese musicians just loved seeing the orchestra here, and they explained that they had been through difficulties during the Cultural Revolution. Some of the musicians had said, "Well, we were sent to work on a fruit farm. But we were given gloves to pick the fruits with." So, somebody was taking care of them. But there were others who had much more hardship, and they [had] suffered during the Cultural Revolution.

Li of the Central Philharmonic presents Ormandy with Chinese instruments, including a pipa, a four-stringed instrument. (Photo by Alan Abel.)

Li holds aloft albums recorded by the Philadelphia Orchestra, part of a collection that Ormandy had given to his counterpart with the Central Philharmonic. (Photo courtesy of the Philadelphia Orchestra Association Archives, used with kind permission.)

Tenny: A pianist [told us] they knew his fingers were important, so he was put to work picking peaches instead of digging ditches.

Zhang: Mr. John de Lancie [principal oboist] gave me two records that he recorded himself. He also gave me two small boxes of reeds, six in total. You know, a professional oboist makes his own reeds. You don't use the ones sold in stores. It takes a lot of time and effort, and you're not successful every time. Probably the best-case scenario is I can get three good ones for every ten I make. When my colleagues and friends heard the news, they all asked for them. I had no choice, so I shared them, but I kept one. It is still with me.

Cui: Everyone was looking at the violin of the concertmaster. It was a world-famous violin that we had never seen, a very beautiful Italian violin. After that, a second violinist, a

Left: Violinist Cui Zhuping *(far left)* with violinist Julia Janson *(third from left)*, whose husband, Glenn Janson, the third horn, was also on tour with the Philadelphia Orchestra. (Courtesy of Julia Janson.)

gentleman with darker skin, called me over. He found a chair and put his scores on it and opened them for me. There were four books, and it was Mendelssohn's *String Quartets*, a complete collection.

Zhang: A whole set of original scores was very rare. At the time, you couldn't find it in China. It was almost too precious to be used.

Zhu: We had scores, but they were ruined during the Cultural Revolution or sold as junk. We had to recover the music by writing it out by hand.

Cui: This American violinist said he had already used the sheet music and pointed out that it had a little stain. I said, "It's okay. This is very, very good."

Facing page: Violinists with the Central Philharmonic gather around concertmaster Norman Carol. (Photo courtesy of the Philadelphia Orchestra Association Archives, used with kind permission.)

Booker Rowe: She seemed to express a desire to play this music, and I said, "Okay, let me give you this. Here's an opportunity for you to get some of your colleagues together and just enjoy. You don't have to play it publicly. You can just enjoy it."

Sheila Platt: The orchestra was elated, as were we all, leaving the place through crowds of clapping kids.

Krell: We all left, feeling slightly embarrassed by the paucity of our gifts, but realizing that this encounter was perhaps the most significant part of the entire trip.

11 | SEPTEMBER 16

The Big One

The orchestra entourage was abuzz: the third concert had been designated "The Big One." Just what that meant, none of the Americans knew for sure—and the Chinese hosts weren't saying. At the time, diplomacy in China was a little like bird-watching, and, as the Americans held up their opera glasses at the concert, they hoped for a rare sighting of a secretive leader. The program included the much-debated Sixth Symphony by Beethoven; Respighi's "Pines of Rome"; Barber's Adagio for Strings; and Yin Chengzong performing the *Yellow River Concerto*.

Nicholas Platt: When we renegotiated the whole itinerary, which we did after [Eugene] Ormandy arrived, they said, "We want to add a concert, and this will be a leadership concert." They had originally agreed to three concerts in Beijing and two in Shanghai. The idea was that this would be a concert in which the leadership attended, and that was really all there was to it. But it had special significance because with the leadership being there, there was an excuse for broadcasting it nationwide.

Francis Tenny: Unlike the other concerts, we had to arrive in place two hours earlier than usual, with no explanation. We arrived at the hall [at] the designated two hours early to find it ringed with masses of police and military guards.

Eugene Ormandy: Suddenly, someone came backstage and said to my wife, "Mrs. Ormandy, will you come with me?"

And she went. Then, I said, "I smell something. Something is going to happen tonight."

I asked all these Chinese friends, and they said, "We don't know, we don't know."

Maestro Eugene Ormandy en route to a concert with his wife, Gretel, described by diplomat Nicholas Platt as "a warm, solid, long-suffering Austrian lady who wound him up in the morning, fed him, brushed his hair, tied his shoes, patted him, told him when he was out of line, made him take naps, fanned him when he was too hot, wound him down, and put him to bed." (Photo courtesy of the Philadelphia Orchestra Association Archives, used with kind permission.)

I said, "Who is coming?"
They said, "We don't know."

Sheila Platt: Nick and I and the deputies and wives were seated into a row just behind two empty rows with name cards thumbtacked to the backs. There were two conspicuous center blank chairs. Just as the TV lights went on, a minion rushed in, clapping two cards into place for Madame Mao and Yao Wenyuan [a member of the Gang of Four].

Ormandy: All of a sudden, everyone stood up, big applause. Through a little hole, I looked, and I saw Madame Mao going with my wife and her whole entourage to her place.

Sheila Platt: Everybody leaped up, and Madame Mao came in clapping, her hands raised, glasses glinting, hair in neat ripples. There was a lot of applause as they settled themselves and were photographed. We all observed the dress—black silk crepe, tucked in front, pleated mid-calf skirt, white leather blunt-toed sandals, and white plastic purse. The

dressmaking details were inconspicuous but present—piping on the collar, covered buttons, a self-belt.

September 17, 1973
From: U.S. Liaison Office, Peking
To: Secretary of State, Washington, DC

Madame Mao was dressed in a formal black version of the dress she wore at the basketball game last June [featuring a U.S. collegiate men's and women's team who visited Beijing], white shoes and handbag, and a small evening wristwatch set in a circle of what appeared to be precious stones. Despite her stylish attire and her gracious and good[-]humored behavior, she did not seem nearly as well as when she appeared at the basketball game. Her complexion was sallow, she perspired quite freely on what was not a particularly warm evening, and she seemed to have lost a little weight.

Jiang Qing, seated front and center behind a white paper reserving her place. Flanking her are Gretel Ormandy and Ambassador David K. E. Bruce, U.S. emissary to China. To Mrs. Ormandy's right are Yao Wenyuan, Madame Mao's close associate and member of the notorious Gang of Four, and C. Wanton Balis Jr., chair of the Philadelphia Orchestra. (Photo courtesy of the Philadelphia Orchestra Association Archives, used with kind permission.)

Nicholas Platt: That concert had special significance because of the leadership being there. Sheila and I sat with David Bruce [the ambassador in charge of the U.S. Liaison Office], watching like hawks. There was full TV and national press coverage given to her presence at the event. The hall was hung with banners reading "Long Live the Friendship between the Chinese and American Peoples" and "Welcome to China Concert Tour of the Philadelphia Orchestra."

Davyd Booth: She was a little, tiny, tiny woman. She sat in the front row. One thing, everybody always watched her to see if she was applauding or acting like she was enjoying the music. Everybody had their eyes sort of focused a bit on her all the time.

Sheila Platt: Madame Mao was, as advertised, a very tough cookie. It was obvious that anyone within thirty feet of her was terrified of her. They were all in a state of high alert. I had the impression that she was always very physically restless. It was hard for her to sit still. She was always passing notes around and talking to the person next to her and so on.

Ormandy: We played, of course, the *Pastoral* Symphony. It was the only time, I may add, that she seemed very happy. It was her wish, of course. We talked about it afterward.

Nicholas Platt: The musicians were required to work from pages that contained a jumble of different bowing and dynamic instructions. They simply watched Ormandy, and out came a flawless performance.

Kati Marton: The orchestra really just performed spectacularly. It got a standing ovation. I'm of a political bent. This was still the Cultural Revolution. People jumped up with sustained applause, and I don't think the Chinese were ready for that—that explosion of applause.

Sheila Platt: Jiang Qing led the applause between each movement of Beethoven's Sixth and talked loudly to Li Delun, conductor of the Central Phil, through the "Pines of Rome." Gretel later said Madame Mao was quite extraordinary, mopping her brow, wiggling, talking, and insisting the piece was about wind in the trees and nothing else, not even a sunrise.

Yin Chengzong: When the orchestra played the *Yellow River Concerto*, I could hear all the details that we wanted from the piece but never heard performed before. We never heard anything like it.

Maestro Ormandy conducts Beethoven's Sixth Symphony, capitulating to pressure from Madame Mao. (Photo courtesy of the Philadelphia Orchestra Association Archives, used with kind permission.)

Sheila Platt: The *Yellow River Concerto* played by Yin Chengzong was a great performance of "method" piano playing with soulful gazes into the air above the piano, grimaces, etc. . . . and evidence of real talent, although the piece itself is hard to love, very schmaltzy and strident at the same time. Mr. Yin played without reference to Ormandy, who kept peering hopefully over his shoulder in vain because Yin only looked at him after he'd stopped playing.

Larry Grika: After Yin played, he came off stage, and about ten of us violinists walked off with him. The stage was too small, very cramped, so we went off to make more room for Yin to play his encore. Yin starts to play, and Ormandy, who's standing backstage with us, went nuts. "What is he doing?! We just played this wonderful program, and he's playing this?! This popular piece?!" Yin played what he had played for [Richard] Nixon when the president came in 1972.

Emilio Gravagno: "Home on the Range!" It's not typical encore material. And I would guess that it was chosen to please the American ear and to play something that we were familiar with.

Grika: Meanwhile, he's playing, and he gets a roaring ovation. Yin comes off the stage, and Ormandy says to him, "That's the perfect piece to have played for an encore."

Nicholas Platt: Ormandy had the good sense to have marches in his repertoire, and he ended every concert with a march. Of course, the Chinese love marches. And so, he taught the orchestra the "Workers and Peasants March."

Ormandy: There was an American couple from Michigan who were pianists, Frances and Richard Hadden. She was born in China, and she knew Zhou Enlai from her childhood. She had visited Peking before us. As she was leaving, Zhou said to her, "Is the Philadelphia Orchestra any good?"

And she said, "I think they're pretty good."

"Shall we invite them?"

She said, "Yes, I would."

He said to her, "Wouldn't it be wonderful if the orchestra would play the 'Workers and Peasants March' or 'San Pei'? This is a number that everybody in China knows." I had only the lead first violin part from Mrs. Hadden. I had it orchestrated.

Booth: When we played that, they went nuts. You immediately could just see them beaming with pride. This was their music that they were hearing with an outside-of-the-country ensemble.

Ormandy: Then I said to myself, "Let them hear our best too." I turned around. I didn't say a word to the orchestra. I started immediately to play "Stars and Stripes [Forever]." We had quite a few Americans there in the audience, and they started to applaud. The Chinese joined them. To the Chinese, it was new. They loved it, by the way.

Sandy Grady: An unlikely old gentleman named John Philip Sousa thundered in and blew the cobwebs out of the night. Eugene Ormandy and the Philadelphians played a brassy, gutsy, cornball, dramatic version of "Stars and Stripes Forever" that surely cracked every Ming vase in China. Ormandy warmed up the Chinese with his first encore, the "San Pei" ["Workers and Peasants March"]. That, they understood. But when Mr. Sousa had his turn at bat—well, it was like comparing rice wine to hundred-proof bourbon. Four piccolo players rose in their white tie and tails to trill Mr. Sousa's march. Then, up popped the ranks of

The headline in the *Philadelphia Bulletin* read, "Madame Mao Steals the Show; Ormandy Doesn't Seem to Mind." Every move of Chairman Mao's wife was noted by American diplomats, who cabled colleagues in Washington, DC, and commented on what she wore and how she reacted to the performance. They were looking for outward signs of where the U.S.-Sino relationship might be heading. (Photo courtesy of the Philadelphia Orchestra Association Archives, used with kind permission.)

the Philadelphians' trumpets and trombones. As they tootled and blared through the old flag-waver, every American in the hall felt his scalp prickle or his eyes dampen. Suddenly, Mr. Ormandy had turned this small corner of China into a Fourth of July parade. You could almost smell the burning fireworks or taste the cotton candy.

Gravagno: That may have been a little bit over the top. Everybody in the orchestra was thinking, "If we're going to play 'Stars and Stripes' for Madame Mao, what must she be thinking? How will she react to it?"

Liu Qi: Their performance was so terrific, beyond description. There were only about two or three curtain calls, and there could have been more if the leaders were not sitting in front. We had to follow the leaders.

John Holdridge, U.S. Liaison Office deputy chief: The audience was thoroughly happy, and especially happy was the conductor of the [Central Phil] Li Delun, who felt that a real break-through in culture and the arts, away from "revolutionary" themes fostered by Jiang Qing, had been achieved thanks to the Philadelphia Orchestra's visit.

September 17, 1973
From: U.S. Liaison Office, Peking
To: Secretary of State, Washington, DC

[Madame Mao] gave Beethoven's Sixth (which she later owned up to having requested) a standing ovation, chatted incessantly throughout the Respighi's "Pines of Rome," paid polite attention to Barber's Adagio for Strings, and seemed moved by Yin Chengzong's vigorous performance of the *Yellow River Concerto*. Yao Wenyuan [of the Gang of Four] was genuinely engrossed throughout, nodding his head in time to the music, and emerged as the Politburo's most obvious music lover.

At reception afterwards, she greeted Ormandy by referring to Philadelphia Orchestra's 1940 benefit concert and stating that this early act of support for the Chinese people made her feel as if they had known each other for a long time. "The Chinese people do not forget their old friends," she continued and then presented Ormandy with an autographed 1870 edition of ancient Chinese melodies in traditional notation that came from her own library.

Sheila Platt: We found ourselves herded to the other side of the theater into a long, narrow lobby with banquette chairs and low tables around the walls, set with plates of melon slices and cakes. Yin came in and sat down next to Ormandy. He told me later Madame Mao immediately started talking about Soviet music and how composer Rimsky-Korsakov was very big on China.

Ormandy: She wanted to know about the orchestra, how we practice, what we do, etc. She was talking about music as one who knows music, very, very, very much.

Nicholas Platt: Happily, she spoke in slow, queenly tones, not as a revolutionary rabble-rouser.

Ormandy: We also had played the "Pines of Rome" by Respighi. As you know, there's a phonograph that is used near the end of a bird singing. You can't have a live bird, so that record is played.

Ormandy at a post-performance reception hosted by Madame Mao. In thanking Ormandy, she mentioned the 1940 concert in Philadelphia to benefit China's relief services during World War II, saying, "China does not forget her friends." (Photo courtesy of the Philadelphia Orchestra Association Archives, used with kind permission.)

She said to me through an interpreter, "That didn't sound natural to me."

I said, "Madame Mao, it wasn't natural."

Daniel Webster: She told Ormandy, "Thank you for this concert. We are old friends. You supported us in the forties, and we are grateful. China does not forget her friends."

Grady: A bit defensively, she talked of the music Ormandy had played—the Philadelphians had been told to avoid Russian music. "We have heard you have the wrong impression that we have many restrictions," said Madame Mao. "The Russian people have many good people, many great musicians and engineers. It is only the Russian revisionists we are against." Ormandy, whose interest in Sino-Russian politics wasn't overwhelming, said, "Music creates quick friendship between people. That's why we are here."

Madame Mao shaking hands with orchestra members. She thanked every musician and gave each a gift—a packet of cassia seeds "to flavor their tea." (Photo courtesy of the Philadelphia Orchestra Association Archives, used with kind permission.)

Sheila Platt: Madame Mao took a package wrapped in white paper from an aide who rushed in with it and presented it to the maestro with a speech about music and friendship. She described the books—limp, paperbound volumes—as rare and from her own library, preludes written down in the 1870s, although many were older than that. She said that having been busy with revolution, she had forgotten all she ever knew about "bean sprouts" (traditional Chinese musical notation). Next, Jiang Qing drew from her purse a polyvinyl envelope of what she described as "cassia flowers" gathered in her own garden by her. These were to be given [to] the musicians "to flavor their wine and put into cakes."

Tenny: After an extended time, she rose and commanded, "I want the musicians back so that I can talk to them." A Chinese official took off at once for the hotel.

Anthony Orlando: There were at least four buses. A police car came from behind with sirens blaring and stopped our bus, just before we got there. The police came in, and they talked to the driver. They asked to turn the bus around and not stop at the hotel. Several of my colleagues became very frightened and ran off the bus, shouting, "You're not going to keep me from getting off this bus! I'm from America. I'm from a place that's a free country." They got off. I don't know what they thought was going to be happening.

Grika: One fella says, "I've got to go back! My wife is calling me at a certain time, and I have to be there."

He was told, "Impossible, you have to go to the party. Madame Mao's throwing a party, you have to be here."

"No, I have to leave. I'm sorry, you have to take me to my hotel."

And they conferred with some other people and finally said, "Yes, we're going to take you to the hotel and after the call, you're coming immediately back to the party."

John Krell: Very imperious and very much a power, she wished to have pictures taken with us. So, bleachers were hastily assembled, and Madame Mao personally greeted each member as we left and gave each a packet of fragrant cassia seeds that she had picked from her garden.

Renard Edwards: I remember being in the reception line with her, and I had memorized the word for *thank you*. And because she was giving out packets of these very small flowers, when I got to her, I said, "*Xie xie.*" And she drew back, and she said, "Oh, you speak Chinese?"

Nicholas Platt: After a mineral-water toast, the entire party returned to the stage for mass photographs. Ormandy, on the verge of tears by this point, received another jolt when Madame Huang Chen, who had served as a diplomat in Budapest, approached and addressed him in Hungarian.

Grady: The State Department guys were doing cartwheels. They told me that Madame Mao, appearing with Yao Wenyuan [of the Gang of Four] at her right, put the stamp of approval last night on U.S.-China chumminess.

"After the Cultural Revolution in 1966, they were the hard-line radicals," one said.

He did not smile when I suggested that Madame Mao was a sort of Barry Goldwater in a black 1938 dress from Wanamaker's budget store.

Following page: Musicians and guests pose on stage with Madame Mao. Buses carrying the orchestra members back to their hotel were stopped by police and sent back to the concert hall at Madame Mao's request. (Photo courtesy of the Philadelphia Orchestra Association Archives, used with kind permission.)

News of the Day

Musicians awoke to a front-page story about the concert in the *People's Daily*, the mouthpiece of the governing Central Committee of the Chinese Communist Party. The newspaper ran a photograph of Madame Mao and other Chinese VIPs, surrounded by all 130 visitors from Philadelphia. The state-run New China News Agency, meanwhile, sent a report over the wires that prominently mentioned that Madame Mao and her right-hand man, Yao Wenyuan, had been in the audience. The writer complimented the seventy-three-year-old Ormandy for his "simple and incisive way of conducting." In a cable to Washington, U.S. diplomats wrote that her attendance at the concert gave a hint of her rank in the pecking order of party leadership (tenth, according to the foreign service handicappers) and presented a tangible sign of improving relations.

September 17, 1973
From: U.S. Liaison Office, Peking
To: Secretary of State, Washington, DC

Madame Mao's presence and unprecedentedly warm welcome for the Philadelphia Orchestra . . . represented strong reassurance that development of bilateral relations with the United States remains a priority item for the Chinese leadership. Her well[-]publicized actions put into perspective the rhetoric of the Tenth Party Congress and other recent ideological statements lumping the United States along with the Soviet Union as a practitioner of "superpower hegemonism." From this standpoint, the orchestra's appearance could not have been better timed. We are waiting, however, to see the effect that Madame Mao's obvious support for

Eugene Ormandy, who had fretted over the initial Chinese reaction to his orchestra, is ebullient after positive reports in Chinese media. (Photo courtesy of the Philadelphia Orchestra Association Archives, used with kind permission.)

this particular cultural exchange will have on a program that, from the direction of the U.S. at least, will be stalled after the orchestra departs.

Anthony Orlando: We were all very excited about the *People's Daily*. It was very special to have that article with a photograph of the orchestra and Madame Mao. We all felt like we were diplomats.

Nicholas Platt: The Chinese people really didn't know the broad context of what was going on between the United States and China, but they knew what was happening right in front of them. They were curious about this American orchestra. I've talked to people since then who said that they were just dying to get tickets, including one person who said that she snuck into the concert and got away with it.

Zhu Gongqi: After the liberation in 1949, the first symphony orchestra to visit China was the Soviet State Symphony Orchestra in 1956. Their performance was quite inspiring. They were rather wild. The style of the Philadelphia Orchestra was different. It combined the wildness of the Russians with the elegance and delicateness of the Europeans. Really amazing.

Orlando: Years later, Tan Dun, the great composer of film and orchestral music, came to conduct us in Philadelphia. It was 2004, and we were performing his piece called "The Map." It was one of the first things he said to the orchestra, how he was inspired by us as a teenager, when he was living in the hinterlands of China.

Tan Dun, composer: I told this story to the orchestra members. I said, "This is the first orchestra I heard, from a loudspeaker in the field. And this orchestra sound, this orchestra—actually, *all of you*—changed my life."

Tan Dun was a teenager in 1973, when, like so many of his generation, he was sent to the countryside in the Hunan Province to work on a commune. Chairman Mao had extolled the country's youth to "learn from peasants." In such remote, rural communes, people did not have access to television or radio. They got their news of the day from morning addresses blasted from loudspeakers.

Tan: I had been sent to a place called Huangjin Commune. I heard a big noise coming from a loudspeaker in the field. A man said, "Do you want to hear some interesting music? This is called 'symphony.' The Philadelphia Orchestra is in China." That was the first time, actually, that I ever heard a symphony orchestra. It was striking. I think it was something by Beethoven—the Sixth or the Fifth Symphony.

Sheila Platt: If you were an ordinary person, you were used to hearing Chinese music or Western instruments playing, like, the *Yellow River Concerto*. But you never heard Mozart or Beethoven.

Tan: Later, I was talking to my grandmother, and I said, "This music is so loud! It holds a pitch so well." Our bamboo flutes or silk-stringed instruments sound like our language. Very

A country road outside Beijing. During the trip, the Americans discovered that musicians from the Central Philharmonic were sent to the countryside to "learn from peasants" during the Cultural Revolution. Composer Tan Dun was a teen, living on a commune in the Hunan province, when he heard a report about the Philadelphia Orchestra's visit coming over a commune loudspeaker, a transformative moment. (Photo by Alan Abel.)

Musicians visited a commune near Beijing. At the time of the orchestra's visit, millions of young people were on communes working among peasants at Mao's direction. (Photo courtesy of the Philadelphia Orchestra Association Archives, used with kind permission.)

lyrical, very dancelike pitch. But this orchestra, this brass, everything, it could be perfect. I was immediately seduced by this orchestra.

Orlando: It was very touching to think that this young kid was out there and that the music had inspired him.

Tan: It was very emotional, very, very powerful. It made me decide: I want to learn this kind of music. I want to compose something for this kind of orchestra! Somehow, the seed of my future was planted after hearing over a loudspeaker a broadcast about the Philadelphia Orchestra during the middle of the Cultural Revolution.

13 | SEPTEMBER 18

Frisbees and Acupuncture

Unlike other foreign tours, the Philadelphia musicians were allowed to be tourists in China—much to Eugene Ormandy's chagrin. On the flight to Shanghai, an irritated maestro complained to Sandy Grady, the *Bulletin* columnist, that he wanted more concerts, less sightseeing: "If the trip is costing $200,000, I want our music to be heard by more people." But once on the ground, Ormandy again acquiesced. He went shopping with his wife. He played tourist. He enjoyed himself. In between concerts, the orchestra visited the Forbidden City, the Summer Palace, and the Red Star Commune. On their sixth full day in Beijing, the entourage traveled forty miles northwest to the Badaling section of the Great Wall.

John Krell: Despite a day off, we were up at sixish to observe the busy street scene from our fifth-floor balcony. Chinese drivers were in the court below, polishing their cars, and some listening to English lessons on their car radios. The shadow boxers were at it in the adjoining court, and we even heard some comical and strained vocal calisthenics. The constant *ching-a-ling* of the bicycle bells was quite musical. Sausage omelet prepared us for the day's excursion to the Great Wall.

Judith Viner: The Chinese kept us totally occupied so we would not be at liberty to go out on our own.

Edward Viner: They filled our time 100 percent. They didn't want us floating around.

Julia Janson: We were objects of curiosity everywhere we went. When we would ride through the streets in our buses, people would be lining the streets, clapping and waving. I

The Philadelphia Orchestra's caravan of cars and buses on a sightseeing trip. Conductor Eugene Ormandy and his wife, Gretel, would travel in the lead car with a personal guide and translator. Such group excursions were unheard of during the orchestra's other world tours. (Photo by Edward Viner.)

remember asking, "Who are these people?" I was told, "They're the clappers. They were told to come out and clap." I felt like the queen of England waving to everyone.

Judith Viner: There was a caravan everywhere we went. Ormandy was always first, in a limousine with a driver and a translator and his wife. In the next car was Richard Bond, the president of the orchestra, and [C. Wanton Balis Jr.], chairman, and their wives. Then, the doctors [including Ormandy's friend, the orthopedic surgeon Irvin Stein] and me. Then, the orchestra in three or four buses. Then, the press in a minibus.

Edward Viner: The caravan could not move until we were all in our right places.

Margarita Csonka Montanaro: Every time we took a trip, they would insist you would have to enter by rank. I thought, "This is Communism." Every single time, every time we went to dinner, walked into a room, we had to walk in order.

The Philadelphia Orchestra's entourage leaves the Dingling mausoleum, one of thirteen imperial tombs that are part of an area known as the Ming Tombs, north of central Beijing. (Photo courtesy of the Philadelphia Orchestra Association Archives, used with kind permission.)

Krell: Our cavalcade took us through newer parts of the city. The suburbs changed quickly to beautifully organized plots of lettuce, corn, etc. . . . where the peasants were going about their tasks with a quiet and unhurried purposefulness. The road narrowed in a steep climb up the mountains to the northwest [part] of the city.

Edward Viner: For most of the trip, the musicians were not interested in seeing me. They were too busy enjoying themselves. But on the way to the Great Wall, one of the cellists had abdominal pain. It had started on the way out there. His belly was quite sore, and I was very concerned. I thought, "What am I going to do with this guy if we're forty miles from the city?" He's writhing and moaning. I did what you are never supposed to do—I gave him a shot of morphine and hoped for the best. He fell asleep. And it went away. I only had one minute on the Great Wall because I was with him in the car.

Anthony Orlando: We were the only people on the Great Wall of China that day. Now you go, it's like going to Disney World, with tour buses, tourist kiosks, and restaurants.

Judith Viner: Most of the wall was rubble. Ormandy didn't do much climbing.

Krell: Its massiveness was impressive, as it literally snakes its way off to the horizon over and around mountains. Most of the orchestra attempted the exceedingly steep climb to the highest two-storied watchtower for a wonderful panorama of the surrounding country.

Sandy Grady: Chinese graffiti [was] everywhere on the wall. Inevitably, a South Philadelphian scratches "Vote for Rizzo" into eight-hundred-year-old granite.

Eugene Ormandy: The fantastic wall, it's just a great experience. You didn't live unless you were there and saw it.

———

Nicholas Platt: With Ormandy, another thing I had to deal with was this business with food. We had all been told he never ate anything but chicken and steaks cooked by his wife in his room. He had said to me, "That's what I eat. That's who cooks." And I said, "Well, the thing to remember is that virtually all of Chinese social life takes place around a table. And if you don't want to meet any other Chinese, or if you don't want to have a social life during this visit, don't come to dinner. But if you do come to dinner, and you can just have a little, tiny bit, that's all that's necessary. And you will meet people, and you will have fun, and you will enjoy it." Well, he did, of course. He liked the food a lot and ate lots of it. But that was his mindset coming in.

Sheila Platt: On a tour of the city in our car, we went shopping at Liu Li Chang, the maestro coatless and pink of face, strolling in his elevator shoes and requiring complete concentration on *him*. You know, he played Beethoven's Sixth. He went to the Great Wall. He ate Chinese food. He emerged from his room all the time, and he ate with other people. He was terrific.

Nicholas Platt: The maestro was much taken with Sheila, her knowledge of Chinese, and her understanding of music. Given to kissing the cheeks of women he admired, Ormandy made a couple of tries, straining on the tips of his elevator shoes (she was more than a foot taller),

Facing page, left: Cameras always at the ready, musicians spend a day touring the Summer Palace. (Photo courtesy of the Philadelphia Orchestra Association Archives, used with kind permission.)

Facing page, right, top: Clarinetist Ronald Reuben (left) greets John Simonelli, French horn. (Photo courtesy of the Philadelphia Orchestra Association Archives, used with kind permission.)

Facing page, right, bottom: Ormandy, not usually one for sightseeing, happily tours the Badaling section of the Great Wall with his Central Philharmonic counterpart, Li Delun. (Photo courtesy of the Philadelphia Orchestra Association Archives, used with kind permission.)

Glenn Dodson, a trombonist, catches a Frisbee, a novelty in China, to the delight of a big crowd of young onlookers. (Photo courtesy of the Philadelphia Orchestra Association Archives, used with kind permission.)

then asked her straight out to bend her knees next time. Naturally she did, and together they formed a new Mutt and Jeff act.

Ormandy: I must say, while we were there, there wasn't a minute where they were not the perfect hosts. We had three or four banquets in our honor, and each was so carefully planned. There were eight to ten to a table, and we had twelve-course dinners. Everyone had several helpings. My wife and I sat at the head table, [and] suddenly a group would stand up and start to toast each other and drink to friendship. Violinist to violinist, trombone player to trombone player.

Nicholas Platt: I remember the ease with which the musicians bonded. They did what came naturally. They reached out. And one of the first things they did in a natural fashion was play Frisbee.

Janson: It took a while for the Chinese to take part in the Frisbee. They weren't sure if they were supposed to. Everything they did had to be cleared with authorities. We took over smiley pins and gave them out to people. They didn't put them on right away because they had to ask if it was okay. They asked if it had hidden meaning.

Alan Abel: We took a whole lot of Frisbees with us. When we would go to different places, like the Great Wall, we'd pass them out to kids and adults to have a good time.

Grady: Back at the Qianmen Hotel, Mr. Glenn Dodson [trombone] yelled, "It's Frisbee time!" It turned out to be a call for mayhem. Dodson, trumpeter Don McComas, trombonist Dee Stewart, and I began tossing the Frisbees, leisurely, in a big concrete courtyard of a cultural hall. The kids had obviously never seen a Frisbee. They watched, pop-eyed and shy. They got into the game. Suddenly, it was chaos. We had fifty kids. Then one hundred, then three hundred. Traffic was piling up on the Yung Lu Avenue. This mob of kids, eight to thirteen years old, was creating China's first Great Frisbee Riot. "Wasn't that great?" said Dodson. "I'll bet the Chinese will have engineers trying to build their first Frisbee tonight. Man, that's what this trip is about—people to people."

The medical professionals on the tour—the Viners and Dr. Stein—told Ormandy that they wanted to visit a hospital. The Chinese hosts arranged for them to go to the Friendship Hospital to observe an operation on a woman, who underwent surgery using only acupuncture—no anesthesia.

Robert de Pasquale: Dr. Viner knew my shoulder was bothering me, and he knew I was interested in acupuncture. He said, "Listen, I'm going to see an operation. Would you like to come with me?"

Edward Viner: It was in an amphitheater. We sat about ten feet above the operating table, looking down. I could see no IV lines on the patient. She wasn't hooked up to anything.

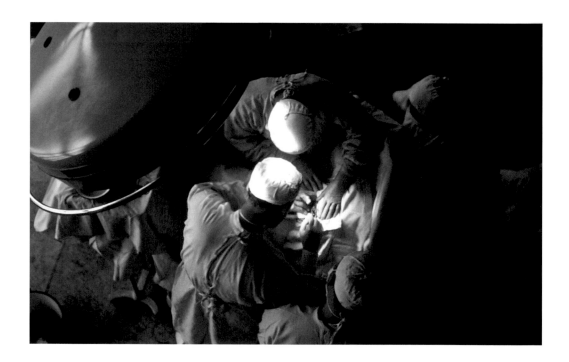

Chinese surgeons remove a tumor from a woman who only received acupuncture as anesthesia. The orchestra's physician, Edward Viner, led a group of musicians to the Friendship Hospital to observe the surgery. (Photo by Edward Viner.)

De Pasquale: There was an acupuncturist sitting next to her with needles. The woman was talking to him like he was having tea with her. The surgeon sliced her from the front of her chest to the back. As he's cutting, the woman is still smiling and talking to the acupuncturist. He pulled out what looked like a small watermelon.

Edward Viner: She had a benign tumor. They hadn't given her any local anesthesia.

De Pasquale: She was wheeled out of the room, and she's still smiling. I can't believe what I'm seeing.

Edward Viner: After that, all the musicians wanted to try acupuncture.

Judith Viner: Everybody was so interested in it. They were overwhelmed with requests. Our hosts decided it would be most convenient for everyone just to have a doctor come to the hotel. They set up a clinic in one of the rooms for an acupuncturist [Dr. Chang Xuwen].

De Pasquale: I had a constant, chronic stiff pain. Aspirin did not help, it was too severe. My neck was so bad it was hard for me to put my chin on the violin. It hurt like hell. And no one was allowed to manipulate it anymore because it would have caused more damage. I was heading for surgery. I said, "You know, Doc, I want to have acupuncture."

Edward Viner: All the violinists have sore necks and cervical spine problems. I felt that I had found out enough about acupuncture to say it was worth a try. It seemed safe enough.

De Pasquale: I went to see the acupuncturist, and I walked out feeling much better.

Daniel Webster: The violinist looked like a well-stuffed pincushion. Dr. Chang inserted several needles in the back of his neck, almost at ear level. Two more were jabbed in his shoulders and two more in his upper arm. Other needles protruded from his points in de Pasquale's hands and elbows. Occasionally, Dr. Chang twirled the needles in place.

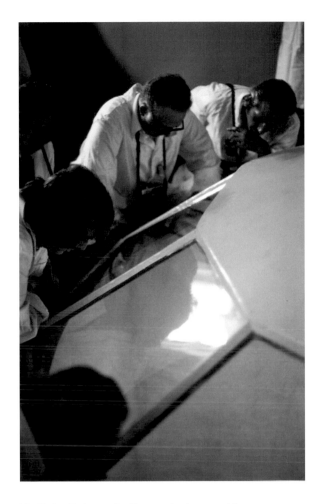

Violinist Robert de Pasquale *(second from bottom)* peers into the operating theater. He decided immediately to try acupuncture to address his chronic pain. He became a convert and relied on acupuncture for the rest of his music career. (Photo by Alan Abel.)

Emilio Gravagno: So many people wanted to try it that they even had an acupuncturist come backstage. At intermission, people would line up and get a two-minute treatment. Maybe 25 percent of us tried it. I had tennis elbow, which was really bothering me. He worked on me for a couple of minutes, and it went away. Almost everybody said they got good results from it.

De Pasquale: When I came back to the States, I had to find people who could do acupuncture. I found someone in Philadelphia. I could go for six months. It was so wonderful that I didn't have to have an operation. To me, the most important thing was I was able to continue playing.

Next Stop, Shanghai

On Wednesday, the morning the entourage departed for Shanghai, two influential newspapers gave the musicians from Philadelphia a send-off that left little doubt of the tour's success. Francis Tenny told the *Bulletin*'s Sandy Grady, "It's almost unprecedented for a United States group of any kind to get this official publicity." A reporter for the *Guangming Daily*, one of the country's top three newspapers and considered the favorite of the educated elite, wrote:

> During these beautiful days the Philadelphia Orchestra has arrived in our country bringing with them the friendly voice of American people to Chinese people. Their warm performance and friendly sentiments conveyed by their performance have left deep impressions on us.

And on Beethoven:

> Beethoven's Sixth Symphony is a piece well known and loved by the music lovers of our country. The Philadelphia Orchestra performed this music vividly.

In the *People's Daily*, a musician for the Central Philharmonic was equally complimentary of the four concerts in Beijing and praised Madame Mao's preferred Sixth Symphony of Beethoven as well as a performance of the Fifth Symphony at one of the concerts. On the Fifth, the reviewer noted:

> His [Ormandy's] treatment of the symphony was well organized, forceful and passionate, especially in the bridge passage between the third and fourth move-

ments. The volume and strength increased step by step until it reached its climax. The orchestra performed a magnificent song of victory with brilliant effect.

And on Respighi's "Pines of Rome":

[It] was like an oil painting in strong colors and clear composition. It portrayed the beauty and grandeur of the Roman city and countryside from various angles. The performance of the orchestra was brilliant in its variation of tunes. The fourth movement was stormy which makes this work into something special on the program.

Nicholas Platt: The leadership had blessed the tour, political tension was gone, and the orchestra musicians simply enjoyed themselves.

John Krell: Everybody flushed out of the Peking Hotel early for the bus to the airport. Porters then appeared with forgotten or discarded items—in my case, a small flash unit for my camera and a damp (but laundered) Honolulu washcloth that I had intended to leave behind. It was a short flight to Shanghai aboard a somewhat crowded Russian plane.

Sheila Platt: We got to the airport at 8:30 A.M. to start the process of sending off the orchestra. Soon, the orchestra poured into the airport, laden with bundles and the Chinese instruments they had been buying. *Youyi*—friendship—was thick in the air, and we escorted them into the plane and waved them off into the sky.

Nicholas Platt: I flew with the orchestra to Shanghai; Sheila traveled separately to meet me there. I sat with the pianist Yin Chengzong. He described the Cultural Revolution and its effect on his activities. At one point in 1967, he said, the "ultra-leftists" [had] launched a campaign attacking the piano as an expensive instrument irrelevant to the needs of workers, peasants, and soldiers. Yin and his supporters countered by loading a piano on a truck and putting on an impromptu concert in Tiananmen Square, which drew an enormous and appreciative crowd and defended his position. Madame Mao, he said, provided strong support at several junctures, arranging at one point for Chairman Mao to attend one of his concerts. When this was publicized, attacks on the piano ended.

Daniel Webster: Anyone who ever doubted the value of a good review should have been with the Philadelphia Orchestra when it landed. The long route eastward into the city along Hongqiao Street and Yanan Road was lined with thousands of people applauding.

Sandy Grady: The crowds along the streets—and this goes on for three days—are intoxicating in Shanghai. Sure, Chairman Mao's word is out to welcome the Americans. But those kids rushing up from the alleys, cheering and waving, have to be spontaneous. Hamlike, I can't resist hanging out the bus window to harangue crowds of two hundred on corners: "Vote for me and I promise honest government!" (cheers) "I'll end the income tax!" (cheers) "I say, let's throw the rascals out!" (bedlam) Says Dan Webster of the *Inquirer*: "A little more work and I think we can carry this ward."

The Philadelphia Orchestra arrives at the Hongqiao Airport in Shanghai after getting rave reviews in China's national newspapers. (Photo courtesy of the Philadelphia Orchestra Association Archives, used with kind permission.)

Judith Viner: Beijing was very gray, with lots of little alleyways and homes built around courtyards. We didn't realize how depressing it was until we got to Shanghai.

Grady: The musicians debate over which city they preferred. Peking was sunny, open, unsophisticated, with the feel of Kansas City with Mao pictures; Shanghai, with a much larger population [of] eleven million, had narrow, crowded, gray streets and the fast tempo of New York City. Manager Boris Sokoloff could only wish the popularity and packed audiences of China could be transferred to the States.

Louis Hood: Sweeping into the gates of the Jin Jiang Hotel courtyard, the musicians found a large knot of applauders clustered at the gate, and with changing personnel and some fluctuating in numbers, they continued their "orchestra watching" until the day of departure.

Krell: The afternoon was filled with a trip to the Children's Palace—truly a remarkable extracurricular effort to teach children under sixteen the arts, crafts, and vocational skills. A charming little girl led our group through a machine shop, electronic circuitry, fertilizer lab, model ship and plane shop, radio shop, acupuncture study group (one girl with two needles in her nose for a cold), herb culture, telegraphy, a playroom, calisthenics, ping-pong practice, ballet, instrumental instruction, sewing, etc., etc.

Above: River traffic on the Huangpu. The art deco Shanghai Mansions apartment complex (formerly the Broadway Mansions) looms in the background. (Photo by Alan Abel.)

Facing page: Eugene Ormandy scans the Shanghai cityscape from the rooftop of the nineteen-story Shanghai Mansions hotel, with its view of the Bund, the city's famed waterfront. (Photo courtesy of the Philadelphia Orchestra Association Archives, used with kind permission.)

Shanghai's Musical History

In the Beijing versus Shanghai rivalry, Shanghai can boast a longer tradition in classical music than the capital city can. As a busy international port with pre-1949 settlements controlled by British, French, and American residents, Shanghai was a hub of Western classical music dating back to the late nineteenth century. In 1879, the Shanghai Public Band, a predecessor to the Shanghai Symphony Orchestra, was founded as the first Western-style orchestra in China, making it older than many notable orchestras in Europe and America, the Philadelphia Orchestra (founded in 1900) among them.

Originally, the orchestra employed only foreign musicians, including many from the Philippines, and performed mostly for foreign audiences. Gradually, interest in the music began to expand among Chinese audiences, and in the 1920s, the first Chinese musicians were allowed to join the orchestra. Many had been educated in missionary schools, where Western instruments were taught.

In 1927, the Shanghai Conservatory of Music opened its doors as the first music institution of higher learning in China. In the 1930s, as refugees from Europe and Russia poured into Shanghai, many Western musicians were included in their ranks. Several joined the faculty of the conservatory. Today, Shanghai boasts the Shanghai Symphony as well as the Shanghai Philharmonic, a frequent collaborator with the Philadelphia Orchestra.

Larry Grika: We had two wonderful ping-pong players. One was a percussionist, Mickey Bookspan; one was a first horn, Nolan Miller. At the Children's Palace, there were kids, and someone asked, "Anyone want to play?" And our two great ping-pong players volunteered. Mickey scored only five points; the other scored only three against these kids. They were virtuosos of ping-pong.

Bernard Garfield: They played five-year-olds and got whipped!

Hood: In between, the Chinese youngsters were charming and talented, and the Philadelphia Orchestra heard "America the Beautiful" again, this time played by an ensemble of nine young girl pipa players.

Krell: We had to rush to get dressed for another big welcoming banquet. Most extravagant menu: hors d'oeuvres, fried shrimp, braised chicken in wine sauce, spring rolls, minced

Applauding children welcome the Philadelphia Orchestra to the Children's Palace in Shanghai. (Photo courtesy of the Philadelphia Orchestra Association Archives, used with kind permission.)

chicken with corn, peanut cakes, stir fried and fried Mandarin fish, soup served in sculpted gourds and chestnut cakes. By now, the toasts dwelling on friendship, success, and cultural exchange have become a litany.

Robert de Pasquale: *Maotai*—boy, did that knock the hell out of you.

Grady: *Maotai* is this country's most dangerous invention since gunpowder. It is a colorless liquor, tastes like cigarette lighter fluid, and has the zap of a Joe Frazier left hook. Regret to say, I was on the Philadelphia Orchestra drinking team that met the Shanghai Revolutionary Committee in a *maotai* contest. Despite strong work by the trombone section, we lost again, 130–0. My opponent at the banquet table was Mr. Gu Boji. . . . Politely, I asked Mr. Gu, through an interpreter, which American author he had read. I realized I had fallen into a trap, when he jumped up, glass in hand.

Above left: Maestro Ormandy listens intently as students perform on traditional Chinese instruments at the Children's Palace in Shanghai. (Photo courtesy of the Philadelphia Orchestra Association Archives, used with kind permission.)

Above right: Raising a toast at a banquet—a familiar sight during the tour. At a restaurant, Philadelphia musicians (*left to right*: Seymour Rosenfeld, trumpet; Nolan Miller, French horn; and Don McComas, trumpet) with their Chinese counterparts. (Photo courtesy of the Philadelphia Orchestra Association Archives, used with kind permission.)

"To Mr. Edgar Snow, the famous American historian, *ganbei* (cheers)!"

"To Mr. Herman Melville, the famous American outdoor writer, *ganbei*!"

"To Ernest Hemingway, the famous American bull-fighting writer, *ganbei*!"

. . . I knew the Philadelphia Orchestra team was in deep trouble when Mr. Gu began drinking to the health and friendship of great musicians.

"To Beethoven!"

Ganbei!

"To Wagner!"

Ganbei!

"To Louis Armstrong!"

Ganbei!

. . . The Philadelphians wobbled to the hotel, singing "Home on the Range" badly off-key.

Sidewalk Serenade

In Shanghai, the musicians stayed at the storied Jin Jiang Hotel, a pair of brick Tudor-style apartment buildings built in 1929 and 1934 by the wealthy Baghdadi businessman Victor Sassoon. After the 1949 Liberation, the buildings were converted into a hotel for party officials and international visitors, including President Richard Nixon in 1972. On the grounds of the hotel, Nixon signed the historic Shanghai Communiqué, which paved the way to normalizing relations with the People's Republic of China. During their three days in Shanghai, Eugene Ormandy and his wife stayed in the same suite as the Nixons had. Just beyond the gates of the hotel, musicians could explore the narrow, shaded streets of what used to be the French Concession.

The Jin Jiang Hotel in Shanghai. Crowds gathered regularly outside the gates of the hotel to catch a glimpse of the musicians. (Photo by Alan Abel.)

Sheila Platt: The Jin Jiang Hotel, in the same grassy compound as the State Guesthouse, is, like the guesthouse, a skyscraper. Shanghai is all art moderne, art deco, built in the twenties and the thirties, and the hotel is a splendid specimen, with curry-colored tiles on the hall walls, gleaming white plaster, and unexpected peach- and aquamarine-colored slipcovers everywhere. The waiters were smart and snappy, and the whole place seemed quite uncharacteristic of this country at the moment.

Robert de Pasquale: I was in the lobby of the hotel, and Harold Schonberg of the *New York Times* says, "I'm going for a walk. Do you want to join me?"

Along the Bund by the Huangpu River in Shanghai. (Photo by Alan Abel.)

Kati Marton, WCAU reporter: I was on that walk too. Harold had a wicked sense of humor and was completely irreverent. We always sat next to each other at the concerts. And he'd say, "Listen to this movement, listen to this." He was like a tutor.

Nicholas Platt: He was blunt to a fault, making sure to tell Yin Chengzong, the Chinese pianist, that the *Yellow River Concerto* was "trash." Yin happened to have been one of the members of the committee that wrote the piece. When upbraided for his rudeness, Schonberg replied, "I'm a frank guy, I'm a frank guy."

De Pasquale: Schonberg was one of the smart critics. Some called him arrogant, but in music, you have to have that kind of attitude. We started walking, and Harold was telling me how wonderful it was to be in this country, when we heard a violin. We didn't know where it was coming from. We stopped and listened. The violinist was playing, I think, first-position scales. It turns out it was a boy of about eight who was standing on a balcony of a house in an alley. I said to Schonberg, "We've got to get this kid to come down. I'd like to talk to him." So, we waved him down. A crowd started to gather on the sidewalk. People were really interested in what was happening.

Marton: Bob tuned the boy's instrument and gave him some pointers.

De Pasquale: We didn't have a translator, but in music, you don't need a translator. I said to the boy, "Play something for me." I corrected some things and told him he should practice his scales and use his bow a little more freely. I said, "This is the way your bow should work, this is the way your fingers should work." I grabbed his fiddle, and I showed him what I wanted him to do. I showed him *legato* playing, when you play two notes together without stopping. I gave him back his violin, and he started to copy what I did. He was so proud and absolutely very serious. Then, I took the violin back and said, "If you practice, you can play things like

Houseboats crowd Suzhou Creek in the heart of Shanghai. (Photo by Alan Abel.)

this." And I ripped into some Sibelius and the first movement of Bach's G Minor Sonata. Everyone gathered around us. Their faces said, "What is this?!" They hadn't heard anything like it.

Marton: We created a little bit of a scene there on the sidewalk. There were looks of absolute wonder on people's faces. This was a sound like nothing they had ever heard, coming from the hands of a master violinist. They were immediately caught up in it.

De Pasquale: There were maybe fifty people or more, gathered around us. The boy ran back to his apartment and grabbed some sheet music. Nobody left. They stood there waiting. He played the music for me. Then, he bowed, and I bowed, and everyone clapped. I think Kati took a Polaroid photo of us, which, of course, everyone wanted to see.

Marton: The theme of the whole trip was the language of music, how it crosses all divides and all barriers. Whatever the Cultural Revolution was trying to achieve was undone in that moment of unfettered communication between culture and generations.

De Pasquale: That was the highlight of my trip. You never expect something like that to happen. We were just taking a walk around the neighborhood. You could tell through the boy's eyes how much he appreciated what was going on. World leaders should have been there watching this. This is what it's all about.

––––––––––

The first of two concerts in Shanghai was held before 1,860 people at the Auditorium of the Revolutionary Committee. The line-up was what became known as "Madame Mao's program," featuring Beethoven's Sixth.

Louis Hood: The shell onstage had a ceiling of curved wooden baffles, and the side walls, although only extending halfway up, were also curved sections, giving a striking resemblance to the set used at the Academy of Music in Philadelphia. The sound produced "out front" was exceptional.

Nicholas Platt: Shanghai audiences were much more alive than those in Beijing.

The audience at a Shanghai concert, as seen from the rear of the stage by percussionist Alan Abel, an amateur photographer who carried his camera everywhere. (Photo by Alan Abel.)

Sheila Platt: One concert had a more musical audience. They were thrilled beyond belief. You can imagine. They had been remembering music, remembering how to play.

Julia Tsien, former pianist for the Shanghai Lyric Opera: I was twenty-four at the time, and the government had assigned me to be an accompanist for singers with a lyric opera company. All we were allowed to perform were revolutionary operas approved by Madame Mao. For classically trained musicians like me, this period of the Cultural Revolution was like a long drought. Even before the Cultural Revolution, we were only allowed to play études and a few pieces by Western composers, but only for training and improving our techniques. I got a ticket to go to the concert because I was a musician. We went to this performance by the Philadelphia Orchestra like we were worshippers.

The first of two concerts in Shanghai at the 1,860-seat Auditorium of the Revolutionary Committee. A Shanghai pianist in the packed audience described the sound as "heavenly." (Photo courtesy of the Philadelphia Orchestra Association Archives, used with kind permission.)

Hood: One of the most memorable and amusing musical happenings occurred when in the "Pines of Rome," the taped song of the nightingale was heard. A Chinese gentleman a few rows ahead of the official party whipped out a pair of opera glasses and scanned the ceiling at the first bird call, causing quite a few others in the audience to follow his cue.

Tsien: Every seat in the concert hall was taken. Unlike other concerts, the audience was so attentive. We later talked about how the orchestra had such superior musicianship as well as instruments. I remember hearing Beethoven. I never heard such a heavenly sound in my entire life.

Rebels on Pointe

Unlike a typical international tour for the orchestra, this trip was as much about the Philadelphians experiencing another culture as it was about the hosts hearing an American orchestra. In Shanghai, the visitors were taken to a midday performance of a revolutionary ballet, *The White-Haired Girl*. This was one of the limited selection of artistic productions—so-called model operas—that was approved for public performances.

John Krell: In the afternoon, I joined our cavalcade of buses for an excursion to a nearby theater (again, through a corridor of clapping streetside people) for a special performance of the ballet *The White-Haired Girl*, which has had a Broadway-like run for three years by a company of young performers.

Louis Hood: Eugene Ormandy broke a long-standing rule of "no afternoon engagements on a performance day" and attended with the entire orchestra. . . . The caravan of five buses and fifteen cars wound over to the Peking Theater in Shanghai for the event, passing clusters of people applauding them and a dense crowd in front of the theater, which gave a warm welcome.

Sheila Platt: Madame Mao had devised a series of operas, movies, plays, all on revolutionary themes. Revolutionary themes were the watchword for culture. And so, there were plays and operas and ballets like *The Red Detachment of Women*, *The White-Haired Girl*, and so forth. There were about seven or eight of them, and they were all that anybody could see during the Cultural Revolution. But they kept the dancers dancing and the musicians playing.

The Philadelphia musicians, with Eugene and Gretel Ormandy, attend a revolutionary ballet—*The White-Haired Girl*—during their Shanghai stay. (Photo courtesy of the Philadelphia Orchestra Association Archives, used with kind permission.)

Hood: Inside, the already-assembled audience of invited guests also applauded the entrance of the Philadelphians as they took their seats.

Eugene Ormandy: I looked down into the pit when they did this propaganda ballet, *The White-Haired Girl*. It's a propaganda ballet, but beautifully done, beautiful staging, beautiful direction, beautiful dancing, and great acting.

Hood: Two screens on either side of the proscenium flashed on the credits in black Chinese characters on a white background. Program notes were supplied in English in a program insert, but there really was no need to have advanced knowledge of the plot. The meaning of this revolutionary dance drama came across as clear as a bell from the actions. The bad guys wore Mandarin robes or were garbed in black and obviously collaborated with the Japanese. The good people wore peasant or soldier outfits.

The White-Haired Girl

If a swan can fall in love with a prince, as she does in the Russian classical ballet *Swan Lake*, why can't a young peasant woman, so tormented by a despotic landlord that her hair turns white, live happily ever after with a revolutionary rebel? *The White-Haired Girl* is based on Chinese folk tales and legends and was shaped into a full-length ballet in 1965. It became one of the so-called model productions that had Jiang Qing's stamp of approval and was performed over and over again during the Cultural Revolution. As in *Swan Lake*, dancers in *The White-Haired Girl* perform on pointe. But the choreography, while borrowing movements from the classical tradition, is more strident and martial to match the revolutionary theme.

The heroine is a young peasant woman, Xi'er, who is waiting for her father to return home for the Spring Festival holiday. Her father toils as a farmer under the yoke of a cruel landlord. When the father returns home in secret because a debt collector for the landlord is after him, all he can give his daughter as a gift is a red ribbon to tie up her hair. The debt collector tracks down the father, kills him, and seizes Xi'er for the landlord's pleasure as a concubine. Meanwhile, her fiancé joins the Red Army to fight for justice. Xi'er toils like a slave. Treated harshly by the landlord's mother, Xi'er attacks her with a whip and is locked up as punishment. Another maid steals a key to her cell and frees her. Xi'er escapes to the mountains, hides in a cave, and suffers so much that her hair turns white. One night, at a temple near her hiding spot, the landlord shows up to worship and provide offerings with his servants. Catching a glimpse of Xi'er, he thinks that she is a ghost. She hurls a brass incense burner at him, and he flees. Her fiancé and his unit of the Eighth Route Army return to battle the landlord and distribute land to the peasants. He learns of Xi'er's fate and sets out to find her. They reunite and rejoice.

In the ballet, a peasant woman escapes a cruel landlord by fleeing to the hills, an ordeal that turns her hair white. When her fiancé rescues her, they join the revolutionary army. (Photo courtesy of the Philadelphia Orchestra Association Archives, used with kind permission.)

Julia Janson: The principal dancer carried a gun and raised it over her head. This was not *Swan Lake* or *Coppélia*. There was definitely a military-type theme, the clash between the people and leaders.

Francis Tenny: It was melodic and gaudy, telling the story of a heroic young woman who during the Japanese War is cruelly mistreated by her feudalistic Chinese landlord. She flees into the mountains and is rescued by the heroic Chinese Red Army. Waving a rifle, she joins the army in the fight against captors, landlords, and Japanese invaders.

Hood: The plot deals with the girl's struggle to achieve happiness even though adversity has changed her hair white.

Krell: The music has the character of a Broadway musical—Tchaikovsky-like intros, bridges, and accompaniments leading into pentatonic hit tunes and dances. The dancing likewise is an amalgam of old and new, much of the traditional Russian ballet techniques mixed with heroic posturing and acrobatic elements. But in spite of this (ballet story lines are perhaps supposed to be inane), there are poignant moments, humorous touches, obvious skill in dancing, and well-paced production in general.

Hood: Technically, this was a beautifully mounted production, utilizing a rear projection of slides and employing a wide variety of scrims with superb lighting effects. It was, in effect, a mixed-media presentation with solo voices and choral sections sung offstage both live and taped and an excellent live orchestra in the pit. The dancing was uniformly superior, even though one missed the flash of flesh normally seen below a tutu. These revolutionary ballerinas were clad in slacks, and not all that well-fitted, either.

Ormandy: We loved every note, every step of it. The orchestra in the pit was first class.

Hai-ye Ni, cello: I'm from Shanghai, and I was a baby when this happened. But that day, my father was in the audience for that performance. My mother, a cellist, played in the pit orchestra for *The White-Haired Girl*. My parents probably never thought that one day, I was going to join the Philadelphia Orchestra.

Hood: Chinese curtain calls are something else too. The curtains part, and the assembled cast leads the audience in rhythmic applause. The Philadelphia Orchestra musicians were especially enthusiastic and appreciative. Regardless of the "hit 'em over the head" political message, this was a first-rate production with a whale of a lot of artistry going into the staging, musical content, and execution.

The pas de deux from *The White-Haired Girl* features the peasant heroine Xi'er and her fiancé, a soldier in the Red Army. (Photo courtesy of the Philadelphia Orchestra Association Archives, used with kind permission.)

Ormandy joins the dancers onstage for final bows. (Photo courtesy of the Philadelphia Orchestra Association Archives, used with kind permission.)

Tenny: The Chinese had been asking our group to recommend what Chinese performing arts group would be well received in the U.S. "Not this one," we said to ourselves.

———————

That night, the orchestra performed its sixth and final concert of the China tour, featuring the same program as the first performance (Mozart, Harris, and Brahms).

Hood: Falling in love with a city is a common failing when one is a guest, treated royally, paradoxically, in the People's Republic of China. And, to a man, the orchestra fell for Shanghai.

Nicholas Platt: The Shanghai stop was a smash.

"Stars and Stripes Forever" closed the first concert (as pictured here) and the last. Television reporter Kati Marton recalls, "I remember constantly fighting back tears." (Photo courtesy of the Philadelphia Orchestra Association Archives, used with kind permission.)

Hood: [It ended] with "San Pei" and "Stars and Stripes Forever." The Chinese were especially thrilled with the show-biz touch, dating back to Sousa himself, of having the first of the four fife players stand for their "gig" and then the entire brass section stand for the finale to end all.

Kati Marton: I remember constantly fighting back tears. It was so powerful, and we knew it was the last night.

Sandy Grady: A crowd of 1,800 in Shanghai's Revolutionary Hall applauded for almost five minutes after the last encore of the John Philip Sousa march. Later, at a farewell banquet at the Jin Jiang Hotel, Conductor Eugene Ormandy pronounced the nine-day trip through China as "the happiest tour of the orchestra's life."

Before the concert, Ormandy had received a cable from David K. E. Bruce, the top U.S. diplomat in Beijing. At the postconcert banquet at the Jin Jiang Hotel, the orchestra's board chairman, C. Wanton Balis Jr., read the message from Bruce:

> I want you to know how much we at the U.S. Liaison Office and I personally appreciate the remarkable contribution which you and the officials and the members of the Philadelphia Orchestra have made during your visit to the People's Republic of China. As fully anticipated, your incomparable music has thrilled capacity audiences in the two largest communities of this nation. You have communicated the universal language with consummate skill and beauty, significantly furthering the President's objectives of better understanding between the Chinese and American people. More than that, it's evident that you and Mrs. Ormandy and your entire personable entourage have formed friendships here which, I am confident, will be lasting and mutually satisfying.

Marton: There were friendships that were formed that obviously we wouldn't be able to sustain when each of us returned to our normal lives. So, there was this sense of saying goodbye. I also knew we had experienced something we would never experience again in our lifetimes. I was very young, but I knew I had been part of something extraordinary.

17 | SEPTEMBER 22

You Yi, *Friendship*

On their final morning in China, before heading to the airport for the first leg of the flight home, the musicians were treated to a leisurely cruise on the Huang-pu River on the excursion boat *You Yi*, which means "friendship" in Mandarin. An ensemble of Chinese musicians playing traditional instruments serenaded them on the excursion. Catching up with the musicians was an *ABC Evening News* correspondent, Steve Bell. Based in Hong Kong, Bell was embarking on a six-week tour of China with his colleague Ted Koppel and started his assignment by covering the final concert in Shanghai. He caught up with Eugene Ormandy on the river tour for a shipside interview. In his report, Bell framed the visit for the network's national audience through a political spectrum. A month earlier, the Chinese Communist Party held its Tenth National Congress, and China-watchers were anxious to examine and deconstruct this high-profile visit by Americans for signs of the emerging power structure and for hints of the tenor of U.S.-China relations moving forward.

Steve Bell, Hong Kong correspondent on *ABC Evening News*: Because the Philadelphia Orchestra was the first important U.S. group to be hosted by the Chinese since the Tenth Party Congress, the trip was closely watched for evidence of any change in the so-called era of good relations between the United States and the People's Republic.

Eugene Ormandy: I know how much it means to our great country to have come here and bring cultural friendship. This is really the greatest experience our orchestra and I have ever had in our long career with all the tours we have made—and we have made many, they were wonderful—but this is really the most outstanding I have ever experienced.

At the Jin Jiang Hotel in Shanghai, Conductor Eugene Ormandy *(center)* bids farewell to Nicholas Platt, chief of the political section in the U.S. Liaison Office in Beijing. Platt made arrangements for the tour and escorted Ormandy and his wife, Gretel. (Photo courtesy of the Philadelphia Orchestra Association Archives, used with kind permission.)

On a slow cruise on the Huangpu River, musicians enjoy a traditional Chinese music ensemble aboard the tourist ship *You Yi*, or "Friendship." (Photo courtesy of the Philadelphia Orchestra Association Archives, used with kind permission.)

A musician *(left)* performs on a *suona*, a double-reed horn, in a traditional Chinese ensemble, performing for the Philadelphia Orchestra. (Photo by Alan Abel.)

Bell: As one American source here said, "It's the first toe in the water since the Tenth Party Congress, and the water was pleasantly warm."

That afternoon, the musicians departed from Shanghai for Tokyo and a refueling stop before continuing to Fairbanks, Alaska. Because of a foul-up in communications, the musicians had an unplanned, overnight layover there. The entourage arrived in Philadelphia late on September 23.

Nicholas Platt: Boris Sokoloff, the orchestra manager, a sensible, fiftyish Yale man, told me as we parted that we probably had had more contact with Ormandy during this ten-day period than 90 percent of the people associated with him in Philadelphia had ever had. We found Ormandy charming, funny, demanding, egotistical, thoughtful, and childlike. He was narrow in his interests, channeling everything into his music.

ABC foreign correspondent Steve Bell interviews Ormandy during the excursion on the Huangpu River. Philadelphia Orchestra President C. Wanton Balis Jr. stands behind them. (Photo by Edward Viner.)

Sheila Platt: A Pan Am stewardess waved the orchestra onto the plane, and the plane took off into the evening sky just at sunset. It was moving, and we all felt a little alone on the empty tarmac.

Nicholas Platt: One observer noted, "Ormandy really didn't need a plane to get home."

Kati Marton: The mood on the plane was one of absolute elation and real sense of achievement on the part of the musicians and Maestro, a sense that we had made history. There was a greater closeness between Ormandy and his musicians because they had shared something unlike any other experience in their storied careers. They had shared this cultural moonwalk. We couldn't predict the next turn of the political wheel, but we felt we had made a real mark.

Sandy Grady: Ormandy's face is like a beacon on the China Sea. "I gave everything I had," he said. "I even gave my own radio to our interpreter. They are such beautiful people. Never has my orchestra been this happy. Nothing would have stopped me from this. Nothing." In the next seat, Gretel Ormandy was nodding, smiling. I caught a gleam between them: no, nothing, not age or pain, would have stopped this ultimate triumph.

Down with Beethoven

Three months after the Philadelphia Orchestra departed China, the political winds shifted dramatically. The same newspapers that had heralded the concerts and extolled the works of Beethoven and Respighi now condemned them. The composers were caught in a broadside. U.S. diplomats searched for meaning.

John Holdridge: When I went to the office and opened my copy of *People's Daily*, I was confronted on the inside front page with a long article containing a great many Chinese characters new to me. Consulting my Chinese-English dictionary, I finally determined that the article represented an attack on Western "program" music, especially pieces such as Beethoven's Sixth Symphony and Respighi's "Pines of Rome"—the two major pieces on the Philadelphia Orchestra's program—because music such as this "watered down the revolutionary enthusiasm of the masses."

> January 17, 1974
> From: U.S. Liaison Office, Peking
> To: Department of State, Washington, DC

> In our view, article represents continuation and extension of general assault on backsliding in educational and cultural circles. Essence of article is that all music has class content, and those who argue that a particular work of music can be judged on artistic merits alone are simply attempting to cover up the bourgeois, capitalist essence of its content, and by extension, their own bourgeois nature. The article thus is warning to musical circles, yet another segment of the Chinese cultural world, that relaxation following the end of the Cultural Revolution and opening to the West

Conductors Eugene Ormandy and Li Delun exchanged scores during the tour, but months later, Beethoven came under renewed attack in the press. (Photo courtesy of the Philadelphia Orchestra Association Archives, used with kind permission.)

is no license to return to pre–Cultural Revolution patterns of behavior.

There is element of xenophobia in the article's use of Western composers Beethoven and Schubert as bad examples and assertion that Mozart's works cannot be placed on a par with sentiments expressed in a chorus scene from *The White-Haired Girl*. Nevertheless, article concludes that "We do not reject all things foreign" and admonishes people to follow Mao's dictum on "Making the past serve the present and foreign things serve China."

As for article's relationship to [Jiang Qing], we . . . noted with interest fact that on day this article appeared in *People's Daily*, new issue of *China Pictorial* hit bookstores showing Madame Mao with Philadelphia Orchestra.

Nicholas Platt: You always had to watch the cultural pages very carefully. We regarded the Philadelphia Orchestra's trip as a huge plus for U.S.-China relations, people-to-people relations, and so forth. But it was still classical music, Western music, which was still controversial.

Francis Tenny: Beethoven had come under attack again in the Chinese media as a corrupt, capitalist-roader influence to be shunned.

Platt: There was all kinds of factional fighting going on within the leadership. Those of us who were analyzing the press at the time saw it as part of the competition between Madame Mao and Zhou Enlai. Zhou Enlai and his supporters had their daggers drawn, and I think this was considered to be a way that Zhou Enlai got back at Madame Mao for her espousal of Western music.

Holdridge: It seems clear to me that Zhou Enlai had succeeded in gaining enough access to the *People's Daily* to generate this attack, which was patently targeted against Jiang Qing. . . . Jiang

Qing's enjoyment of the lilting melodies in Beethoven's Sixth was surely well known in China's inner party circles; the less-familiar "Pines of Rome" was an added bonus for those seeking an excuse to embarrass her on ideological grounds.

Or could it have been the other way around?

Some China-watchers thought that Madame Mao may have been behind the public attacks on classical music and that the catalyst was bad press during and after the Philadelphia Orchestra's visit. When she finally caught up with translations of the reporting of Harold Schonberg, the *New York Times* music critic, including a particularly harsh review that was published a month after the trip and disparaged the *Yellow River Concerto*, she was livid and directed her anger, according to proponents of this theory, at her rival, Zhou, and his music diplomacy.

Harold Schonberg: The *Yellow River Concerto*, promptly nicknamed the *"Yellow Fever" Concerto* by the men in the orchestra, may be a piece of trash, but it is [a] damned hard workout for the soloist. . . . Chairman Mao has said that the proletariat is the only true judge of what is good art. The result, of course, is to reduce all art in the People's Republic of China to the least common denominator. At best, a score like the *Yellow River Concerto* is movie music.

Daniel Webster: The Chinese assault on Beethoven came so soon after the visit of the Philadelphia Orchestra that echoes of Beethoven's symphonies must still have been audible in the Hall of the National Minorities in Beijing. . . . Westerners should not have expected Beethoven to be taken as a model by the Chinese, but because of those euphoric days when the Philadelphia Orchestra and the Central Philharmonic found such harmony in Beethoven, the reminder of differences came as a special blow.

Premier Zhou Enlai, seen here with President Richard Nixon in 1972, was at the center of the brouhaha over Beethoven unfolding in the Chinese press just months after the Philadelphia Orchestra's tour. Was he the instigator of the renewed attack on Western classical music or the victim? Opinions differ, but the crackdown most certainly reflected Zhou's rivalry with Chairman Mao's wife, Jiang Qing. (Courtesy of the Richard Nixon Presidential Library and Museum/National Archives and Records Administration.)

Kati Marton: It was shattering. I naively thought that this was the beginning of a new friendship and opening. The opening would come, but history does not move in a straight line. There would be setbacks from our side and their side.

International wire services picked up on the backlash against classical music. Agence France-Presse sent out a story on the attack on Beethoven that ran in newspapers on January 15, 1974—the very day that Eugene Ormandy appeared at the National Press Club in Washington, DC, to deliver an hourlong lunch talk and Q&A with reporters about the China tour.

National Press Club moderator: A number of people have noticed a news item today. The French press has first reported that China's party newspaper is denouncing Beethoven and Schubert as bourgeois and capitalist. How do you reconcile that with the warm reception accorded the Philadelphia Orchestra?

Eugene Ormandy: This is a very difficult question to answer. I read that article this morning myself, and I was somewhat flabbergasted because I know exactly how they all felt to us. But this must have something to do with politics, with which I have nothing to do. I'm a musician. And maybe things are shifting from time to time. When I talk to them, they love Beethoven, and I never thought of Beethoven as a bourgeois, or Schubert. They were both starving, starving people all their lives.

Still, that's what they say today. I don't know what happens tomorrow.

19 | EPILOGUE

Ode to Joy

In 2017, on the last day in May, the sun-dappled mezzanine of the National Centre for the Performing Arts (NCPA) hummed with convivial small talk. Well-heeled Chinese patrons of the arts mingled over hors d'oeuvres with American diplomats, musicians, and orchestra benefactors, many of whom had traveled from Philadelphia to join the musicians on tour. As the effervescent French Canadian Conductor Yannick Nézet-Séguin arrived at the reception, the crowd parted as he glad-handed his way to the front. He turned to face the crowd and share a toast with the president of the NCPA, Chen Ping.

The NCPA floats like a crystal bubble in a glistening reflecting pool, just a block from Tiananmen Square's dour, intimidating government buildings. With three theaters under glass, it is a colossal, striking, multi-billion-dollar pronouncement of China's ascent in the realm of arts and culture—an assertion of what diplomats call a nation's "soft power." Not coincidentally, the center opened its doors on the eve of the 2008 Summer Olympics, just as visitors from around the world descended on Beijing. The *Ju Dan*, or Big Egg, sends a message: China is a powerhouse not only in sports but in culture.

This night in 2017 was special. In less than an hour, Yannick, as he prefers to be called, would take the podium to lead his musicians and Chinese singers from the NCPA chorus in Beethoven's Ninth Symphony with its "Ode to Joy" proclamation of brotherhood. The conductor drew everyone's attention as he raised his flute of champagne.

"If Beethoven would have known, many hundred years ago, that one day his wonderful piece would have been performed in China in one of the best halls in the world by an American orchestra, a Canadian conductor, and Chinese vocalists, I think Beethoven would not have believed it, and probably from up there," he said, pointing heavenward, "he is so happy."

Fondly known as the "Big Egg," the National Centre for the Performing Arts rises like a glass bubble in central Beijing. Designed by French architect Paul Andreu, the complex is the largest of its kind in Asia and includes an opera hall, concert hall, and theater. (Photo by Jennifer Lin.)

The crackdown on Beethoven and other classical composers in the wake of the 1973 visit of the Philadelphians did not last. Within two years, Western classical music returned to Beijing with a visit by New Zealand's National Youth Orchestra. Then, in 1976, a cataclysmic event: Chairman Mao Zedong, the father of modern China, died. The shackles came off musicians—and clamped down on the notorious Gang of Four, led by his fourth wife, Jiang Qing. Just weeks after the chairman's death, Madame Mao and her three accomplices, who were blamed for much of the suffering during the decade from 1966 to 1976, were arrested and tried for crimes against the Communist Party. In a show trial, Madame Mao was sentenced to death, later commuted to life in prison. In a final act of defiance, she killed herself in her cell.

With the end of the Cultural Revolution, the ban on Western classical music was lifted. Orchestras were again permitted to perform the works of European composers. Music conservatories reopened and were inundated with applicants. Sheila Melvin, a music historian and coauthor with Jindong Cai of *Rhapsody in Red: How Western Classical Music Became Chinese*, notes that in 1977, the Central Philharmonic commemorated the 150th anniversary of Beethoven's death with a performance of his Fifth Symphony. The last two movements were broadcast on nationwide television—coverage that would have been unthinkable a year earlier. "For music lovers, that's the real end of the Cultural Revolution," Melvin says. "That's when they knew it was over, and it wasn't coming back. You could play Beethoven again."

With this new openness, two small matters that had perplexed the Philadelphians during and after their visit were resolved. One had to do with a glaring omission in their 1973 itinerary: despite requests, they never visited a music conservatory. They were treated to performances by local troupes as well as a closed-door rehearsal with the Central Philharmonic, and they observed young children studying Chinese instruments at the Shanghai Children's Palace. But they never observed the training of professional musicians, never conducted a master class with students, never saw the Chinese version of, say, Philadelphia's Curtis Institute of Music or New York's Juilliard School.

"This was a point of puzzlement to which no one could find an answer," writes Louis Hood, the orchestra's director of public relations, in his account of the trip. The best they got from their handlers was the explanation that conservatories were "revising curriculum"—a stunning euphemism for silenced and shuttered. Classically trained musicians suffered inordinately during the most violent period of the Cultural Revolution from 1966 to 1970 because they represented old, bourgeois ways—exactly what Mao goaded the Red Guards to purge from society. Many esteemed Chinese professors of music had studied with expatriate teachers from Eastern Europe and were pilloried by rabid young rebels for these foreign connections. At the Shanghai Conservatory of Music, seventeen professors committed suicide. This was why the conservatories were studiously avoided in 1973.

The other mystery concerned the Philadelphia Orchestra's genuine desire to present the music of Chinese composers to its patrons. Eugene Ormandy heard the Central Philharmonic perform "Reflections of the Moon on the Second Fountain" and had been impressed with the piece, composed by a blind folk musician, Ah Bing, and orchestrated by the composer Wu

Zuqiang. Maestro requested a copy of the music, but, as Melvin and Cai write, Li Delun, the Central Phil conductor, was forced to evade his repeated requests. He was unauthorized to give a score to a foreigner without the approval of Jiang Qing. By the end of the trip, Madame Mao did give her permission, and Ormandy scheduled the piece for the next season at the Academy of Music. But when Hood later requested program notes, he was met with silence. This was 1974, when the backlash against foreign orchestras and classical music was in full swing. Li had to lie to Hood; he wrote that the arranger of the piece thought his own work had serious problems and did not want it performed.

Then, in 1977, Li directly wrote to Ormandy to apologize. In a typed letter, which arrived at the offices of the Philadelphia Orchestra on September 25, 1977, the Central Phil conductor could finally come clean with Ormandy. He writes in English:

> For your reference, herewith enclosed is some extra material on "Reflections of the Moon on the Second Fountain" and its composer. This work [was] forbidden in 1973 by Jiang Qing and the Gang of Four and their underlings in the Ministry of Culture.
>
> Now that the conspiracy of Jiang Qing and her underlings has been smashed, an excellent situation prevails. There has been a rejuvenation on the stage, in literature, and in art[,] and "Reflections of the Moon on the Second Fountain" is being publicly performed here.
>
> We hope the enclosed material, which Mr. Louis Hood of your orchestra asked for in his letter in 1974, will be useful. Under the circumstances, if you wish to present "Reflections of the Moon on the Second Fountain" in a public concert, we would feel much honored.
>
> My colleagues and I often recall with pleasure your orchestra's visit to our country three years ago and particularly think of our very pleasant meetings together.
> Yours sincerely,
> Li Delun

This period of rejuvenation, as Li called it, was dynamic. A confluence of unique forces—political, economic, cultural, and societal—powered a robust revival of classical music that was, in many ways, unique to China. For starters, the decade of deprivation defined by the Cultural Revolution created pent-up demand for performing, enjoying, and learning Western classical music. "We all felt liberated because we can do so many things that we were not allowed to do before," says Jindong Cai, a conductor and violinist who was a boy in Beijing at the start of the Cultural Revolution. Like many musicians of his generation, he immediately wanted to study music once conservatories reopened in 1978. "We caught Beethoven fever. Every orchestra started playing Beethoven's symphonies. Everyone wants to listen to Beethoven's symphonies."

The musician Tan Dun seized the opportunity to begin his formal training as soon as he could. A violinist, Tan Dun was a teen living in the rural Hunan Province when, in 1973, he heard snippets of the Philadelphia Orchestra performing Beethoven over a commune loudspeaker. In 1978, the Central Conservatory of Music in Beijing reopened its doors, and Tan Dun joined the rush of young applicants. "The Central Conservatory of Music was calling for ten positions for the composer. I said, 'Oh my god, ten! That's a lot!'" Tan Dun recalls. "Over ten thousand people were fighting for these ten positions." Tan Dun was accepted into the composition program, based on the strength of a sample composition, a trio for violin, cello, and harp called "I Dreamed of Mao Zedong." After graduating from the Central Conservatory, he left for New York City in 1986 to pursue his doctoral degree in music composition at Columbia University. Tan Dun and the other members of this first class at the Central Conservatory "became a symbol of the resurrection of classical music in China," says Cai, who started the U.S.-China Music Institute at Bard College. "The most active composers today came from that class."

———

Concurrent with this artistic revival, China's paramount leader, Deng Xiaoping, opened China's economy and ushered in one of the greatest industrial booms in history. Families enjoyed rising incomes and had disposable funds to lavish on their children. Under the government's one-child policy (which has since been lifted), that investment in the next generation became especially focused. The central government, meanwhile, encouraged more funding of music education in schools, reinforcing the aspirations of parents and ensuring that children at an early age were exposed to music.

As the classical-music scene began to revive, the Philadelphia Orchestra retained a special place in the collective memory of the *laobaixing*, or ordinary folks. Nicholas Platt, who in later years served as U.S. ambassador in Pakistan, the Philippines, and Zambia, recalled that whenever he traveled in China in the 1980s and engaged in small talk in Chinese with taxi drivers, if he would say "Philadelphia," the unprompted, automatic reply would be, "Orchestra!"

"You could tell," Platt observes, "this had sunk in pretty deep."

It took the Philadelphia Orchestra twenty years to return to China. The 1993 Asia tour of the orchestra, with stops in Tokyo, Beijing, Shanghai, and Hong Kong, featured a televised concert at the Great Hall of the People, the symbolic epicenter of political power in the Chinese capital. A television audience of eighty million watched as President Jiang Zemin took his front-row seat, along with the Central Phil conductor Li Delun and executives from corporate sponsors Cigna, AT&T, and Coca-Cola. The printed program included calligraphy from Jiang and a greeting from President Bill Clinton. Conductor Wolfgang Sawallisch led the orchestra in works by Schubert and Dvorak. Jiang, an aficionado of classical music, had made it a goal to raise the quality of orchestral music and music education in China.

Among the seven thousand people in the cavernous hall was a promising young pianist from the Central Conservatory who was just shy of his eleventh birthday. Sitting with his father, the boy vowed that one day he would travel to Philadelphia to hear this orchestra at its storied home, the Academy of Music. Lang Lang, whose fame today reaches around the world, got his wish four years later, when he arrived in Philadelphia in 1997 to enroll in the elite Curtis Institute. Every Saturday, he used his student pass to attend orchestra performances at the academy. If there were no student seats available, he'd buy a ticket. Lang Lang studied with the legendary pianist Gary Graffman, who predicted that one day he would share the stage with the Philadelphia Orchestra.

Lang Lang's big break came in 1999, when he was asked to fill in at the last minute for an ailing André Watts, who was headlining a gala with the Chicago Symphony Orchestra at the Ravinia Festival. His performance of the opening movement of Tchaikovsky's Piano Concerto no. 1 left the audience breathless. The headline for the *Chicago Tribune*'s review read, "17-Year-Old Sub Steals the Show at Ravinia Gala." Violinist Isaac Stern, who witnessed his performance, wrote a letter to his friend Graffman: "This is someone special. Take good care of him."

As Lang Lang jokes, the gods were looking after him. Two years later, the Philadelphia Orchestra was returning to China and wanted Lang Lang as its headliner in a concert slated for the Great Hall of the People—another dream come true for the young pianist, now making headlines around the world. But the choice was not well received in Beijing—the Chinese promoters wanted a marquee name and offered alternatives who had recently won high-profile piano competitions. But Sawallisch refused, issuing an ultimatum. "He said to them, 'If you guys aren't going to approve that Lang Lang plays with me, then we're not going,'" the pianist recalls. The orchestra even sent a letter of support from Governor Tom Ridge, calling Lang Lang "our adopted Philadelphian." The Chinese side relented. But soon after, a diplomatic crisis almost derailed the tour. On April 1, 2001, a U.S. Navy spy plane collided over the South China Sea with a People's Liberation Army jet, killing a Chinese pilot. The U.S. crew, after making an emergency landing on China's Hainan Island, was detained by the military. Unlike the goodwill surrounding previous tours, the heated standoff in Hainan risked jeopardizing this fourth tour. But with just weeks to go, tensions eased enough for the orchestra to proceed.

Pianist Lang Lang as a student at the Curtis Institute of Music with his teacher, Gary Graffman. When Lang Lang arrived in Philadelphia in 1997 as a fifteen-year-old, he attended weekly performances of the Philadelphia Orchestra at the Academy of Music without fail. (Photo by David Swanson.)

On June 1, 2001, the nineteen-year-old Lang Lang returned to the Great Hall of the People to make his China debut as a professional. In the front row were his parents and, once again, China's president, Jiang Zemin. "It was quite intense, and until today, I feel so grateful, and so emotional when I think about it," Lang Lang recounts. "To play with the Philadelphia Orchestra in China—in Beijing, my second home—you know, you cannot get any better than that."

———

For many years after the opening of China in 1979, the cultural bridge ran in one direction, with American and European classical musicians and orchestras heading to China to perform. But soon, the traffic started heading both ways. Legions of Chinese students entered U.S. conservatories, and greater numbers of professionals joined top-flight U.S. orchestras. Chinese composers increasingly presented their music to American audiences.

Tan Dun went from busking on New York sidewalks as a struggling graduate student in the 1980s to composing works for such artists as cellist Yo-Yo Ma in the 1990s. The director Ang Lee engaged him to write the score for his 2000 blockbuster, *Crouching Tiger, Hidden Dragon*. Tan Dun was awarded a Grammy and an Oscar. At the Academy Awards, he had been up against Hollywood veterans, including John Williams, Ennio Morricone, Rachel Portman, and Hans Zimmer. After Goldie Hawn handed him his statue, he said, "My music is to dream without boundaries. Tonight, with you, I see boundaries being crossed."

In 2004, Tan Dun conducted the Philadelphia Orchestra performing his piece, "The Map: Concerto for Cello, Video and Orchestra." The composer's hallmark is mixing media; the nine-movement work featured documentary footage of the musical life of ethnic groups in the Hunan Province projected above the stage. "At the end of the concert," wrote the classical music critic for the *Philadelphia Inquirer*, David Patrick Stearns, "came a through-the-looking-glass moment: One of the video musicians, a 25-year-old singer named Long Xian-E, emerged from an aisle seat in Verizon Hall, looking unchanged from the video shot five years ago. She sang two songs, 'Water High Note' and 'Lost Love.' It was unexpected, captivating and incredibly cool. . . . All elements taken together, [the concert] so defied usual contexts, the mind wouldn't accommodate cliched reactions, such as 'Aren't the peasants noble?' I'll be processing the concert for weeks."

If "The Map" shattered conventions, it was merely a warm-up for Tan Dun's monumental work, "Nu Shu: The Secret Songs of Women." The composer calls this thirteen-movement piece, showcasing the harp, "a micro film symphony." His inspiration was a secret language and musical tradition, practiced only by a small group of women in the Hunan Province as a way for them to communicate after leaving home for arranged marriages.

Tan Dun credits his father with encouraging him to explore the *nu shu* culture of women in Hunan, with its secretive language. "I was fascinated that it was spoken from mother to daughter, generation to generation, but disappearing," the composer explains. "I said, 'Why not maybe make a harp a solo instrument? The most effeminate instrument transformed as the most powerful storyteller, with this ancient tradition of secret language of women.'"

Often sung, the *nu shu* language has its own calligraphy, with characters that look like praying mantis insects in different poses. "Women embroider it into pieces of clothing," says Elizabeth Hainen, the principal harpist for the Philadelphia Orchestra. "At a time when

Conductor Yannick Nézet-Séguin and composer Tan Dun confer before the Beijing premiere of "Nu Shu: The Secret Songs of Women." (Photo by Jan Regan.)

women weren't supposed to have much of a voice, this was a way for them to express themselves. Many women were in arranged marriages at an age of twelve or thirteen, and they never saw their families again. But they could communicate by sewing and embroidering things into their shoes, their belts, and their dresses as gifts to send. It was a way for them to keep hold of some of their past with their loved ones."

"Nu Shu," the symphony, was a co-commission between three orchestras on three continents: Japan's NHK Symphony Orchestra, the Royal Concertgebouw Orchestra of the Netherlands, and the Philadelphia Orchestra. The symphony was presented to American audiences for the first time at Philadelphia's Kimmel Center in the fall of 2013, with a China premiere in Beijing set to highlight the Philadelphia Orchestra's 2014 Asia tour. The tour came at a pivotal moment for the orchestra. Chinese audiences would be introduced to the orchestra's dynamic, young conductor, Yannick Nézet-Séguin. And the repertoire, spotlighting Tan Dun's work, would reflect a broader and intentional decision by the orchestra to deepen its presence in China. That focus on China evolved during a challenging period for the orchestra. Battered financially by the 2008 recession, with eroding attendance, a dwindling endowment, and rising costs, the orchestra decided in 2011 to file for protection from its creditors under Chapter 11 of the U.S. Bankruptcy Code. Other orchestras in America were also forced to seek bankruptcy protection to relieve financial pressure, but the Philadelphia Orchestra was the only one of the elite "Big Five" to have to take such a drastic step.

Musicians who had been accustomed to regular swings through Europe, Asia, and South America wondered whether they would ever tour again. But instead of pulling back, the orchestra made the strategic decision to strengthen its ties in China with a multiyear touring commitment. And there was an added element: musicians would fan out into the community for events like pop-up concerts at parks or hospitals, master classes for students of music, and side-by-side concerts with professional and amateur musicians. "We began to think what China might be as a new market, really a second market, an income-producing, but a grounded-in-mission effort to secure touring for the orchestra," explains Allison Vulgamore, the orchestra's chief executive officer at the time. This combination of regular touring, plus outreach into the community, was a way of preserving musical and personal bonds "that help not just classical music audiences in China but our countries hear each other a little differently."

In 2012, a year after its Chapter 11 filing, the orchestra emerged from bankruptcy court with a plan of reorganization as well as this new strategy for China. Vulgamore also had secured another critical piece to the orchestra's future: a new artistic director to lead the way. "We'd been searching for a music director for four and a half years. Yannick was on everybody's dance card," Vulgamore says. "He was music director of Rotterdam. He was conducting Berlin and Vienna, and he was making all of his tours of the United States." The CEO was not the only one courting him, but she was, perhaps, the most persistent. "I learned how to fly from Philadelphia to Amsterdam and get my Starbucks at the airport, hop the train, get to Rotterdam, and walk across the street to his apartment. And I did it every two weeks for about four months. I told him that we were at such a moment of truth about ourselves, that I would do the heavy-lifting on the finances, and when we came out, we needed him to be there."

With every visit to China, violinist Philip Kates takes his music into the community. The orchestra makes a special effort to connect with local audiences through pop-up concerts, master classes, and visits to schools and hospitals. (Photo by Jan Regan.)

Yannick, who took over as artistic director in 2012, had performed in China before with the Rotterdam Philharmonic, but the 2014 tour was his first as conductor of the Philadelphia Orchestra. Then thirty-seven years old, the conductor felt the weight of history on his shoulders. "The starting point was 1973," Yannick noted, "but the way the relationship has now materialized in this extraordinary cultural boom of classical music in China makes us old friends and future leaders at the same time."

Nearly a half century after the Philadelphia Orchestra's historic tour, China has energized the world of music at a time when orchestras in America and Europe have struggled to retain audiences. No one wants to be left behind. The touring schedules of top-tier orchestras the world over include stops in Beijing and Shanghai on their itineraries. While the Philadelphia Orchestra may have been first, it now competes with others for the attention of Chinese audiences. The New York Philharmonic has committed to regular touring and has teamed with the Shanghai Symphony to create an academy for intensive instruction in orchestral

Lang Lang performs Rachmaninoff's Piano Concerto no. 1 before a sold-out crowd in Beijing. (Photo by Jan Regan.)

studies. The prestigious Juilliard School opened a graduate campus in Tianjin. Across China, too, cities have built spectacular new concert halls and added conservatories. In five years, from 2012 to 2017, the number of professional orchestras increased from thirty to seventy-two. The expanded Sichuan Conservatory of Music, founded in 1939, had fourteen thousand students in 2020. The head of Juilliard's preprofessional program, Yoheved Kaplinsky, called the collaborative efforts with U.S. orchestras and conservatories "the most extensive musical exchange between two countries at any point in history."

———————

This raises the inevitable question: Can China save classical music? "China's goal is not to save classical music," author Sheila Melvin asserts. "China's goal is to be a part of the global classical music world and to contribute to the canon with new music as well as performing the old music." For the 2014 Beijing premiere of "Nu Shu," Yannick presented a glimpse of the way forward. The concert, with one of the most iconic American orchestras performing the work of one of China's most popular composers, made national TV news. Stearns of the *Inquirer* described "a rock-star ovation" from an NCPA audience for Tan Dun after his forty-minute "Nu Shu." This was no ordinary symphony. The composer compiled video montages of rural women who spoke *nu shu*—with scenes of them singing, paddling in a canoe, embroidering cloth, preparing for a wedding, and wailing at the thought of impending separation—that were projected on three screens above the stage. He mixed into the score Chinese instruments like bells and sounds from nature like hands slapping water as a kind of liquid cymbals or dripping from fingers for a plucking noise.

The next performance of "Nu Shu," in the capital of the Hunan Province, Changsha, was an emotional homecoming for the composer. The Hunan Grand Theater, which had never hosted such a world-class orchestra, sold out tickets three months in advance. Tan Dun counted family, former teachers and classmates, and friends from his commune days in the audience. "When we took 'Nu Shu' on tour, first to Beijing and then to play it in Tan Dun's hometown province of Hunan, we were not prepared for the reaction," Hainen, the harp soloist, recalls. "We are playing along with women who are singing in this language, but they're not there in physical form. But you feel they're there, and you feel what they were going through, through their stories."

For his bows, Tan Dun took with him on stage the villagers who had been featured in the videos. Wearing traditional indigo tunics over black pants, the women, one or two young but most elderly, stood between the conductor and soloist, resplendent in a strapless red satin gown. "When they came out and I saw these women, who I had felt like I knew in my practice room, it was very touching, very powerful," Hainen says. "This woman told me on stage, she says, 'Now, I have an American granddaughter.'"

The boy in the rice field who heard the Philadelphia Orchestra performing Beethoven a lifetime ago now stood shoulder-to-shoulder with the same musicians on stage in his hometown. The moment for him was overwhelming. "I know how much the Philadelphia Orchestra comes to China to play there. Again and again and again . . . they even went to Hunan! Ah, come on. My hometown. It means they touched the soul of Hunan, they touched the soul of me. If they touched the soul of me, it means they touched the soul of my music."

The year 2017 marked another milestone for the Philadelphia Orchestra, with its performance of Beethoven's Ninth Symphony with the NCPA chorus. As Yannick was working the crowd at a preconcert champagne reception at the Big Egg, an elderly couple hailed a cab to take them to the performing arts center to see him conduct. They lived in a neighborhood on the northern side of Beijing, chockablock with identical, utilitarian housing for socialist-era "work units," or *danwei*. Many of their neighbors were retired musicians like them who had been with the Central Philharmonic back in 1973 when Maestro Ormandy came to rehearse with them.

Cui Zhuping had a career as a second violinist; her husband, Zhang Dihe, played the oboe. Zhang grew up in a musical family. His father was a professor of literature at the prestigious Tsinghua University. The youngest of six, he had two sisters and a brother who also were professional musicians. Surrounded by music, he could hum the second movement of Dvorak's *New World* Symphony by the time he was eight years old. Cui's parents loved to listen to Peking opera. When she was a child growing up in Sichuan, they took her to performances, and while she liked the costumes, she didn't like the piercing sound of the singers. What she preferred was listening to classical music on the radio (permissible before music and art became severely controlled by the government). She learned how to play the violin as a child, went on to the Central Conservatory, and joined the newly formed Central Phil, where she met her husband. The orchestra was started in 1956 at a time when the prevailing belief was that music should be more revolutionary and less beholden to Western culture.

In her living room, Cui kept a treasured memento from the Philadelphia Orchestra's trip, tucked among sheet music on her shelf: four booklets with all the parts of Mendelssohn's *String Quartets*. Her husband also had keepsakes: a single oboe reed from principal oboist John de Lancie and a ballpoint pen that Ormandy handed out to all the Central Phil musicians, inscribed with the 1973 tour dates in English and Chinese.

In 2016, at a reunion luncheon in Beijing for Philadelphia veterans of the 1973 trip and their counterparts with the Central Phil, Cui was happily surprised when second violinist Booker Rowe walked into the restaurant. She hurried up to him and explained how so many years ago, he had given her the Mendelssohn sheet music. "Back then in China, we still had a lot of hand-copied sheet music in our orchestra that we had to copy ourselves," Cui explained

Facing page: In Changsha, the capital of Hunan province, village women featured in the symphony "Nu Shu" share the stage with Tan Dun, harp soloist Elizabeth Hainen, and conductor Yannick Nézet-Séguin. (Photo by Jan Regan.)

Right: Retired members of the Central Philharmonic Society, Zhang Dihe *(standing center)* and his wife, Cui Zhuping *(standing right)*, applaud the Philadelphia Orchestra after its performance of Beethoven's Ninth Symphony in Beijing. (Courtesy of History Making Productions.)

Facing page: Conductor Yannick Nézet-Séguin during the finale of Beethoven's Ninth Symphony at the National Centre for the Performing Arts. (Photo by Jan Regan.)

through a translator to Rowe. "I was very excited to get this music. I remember this very clearly. It was given by you." Rowe beamed.

The following year, during the 2017 China tour, Cui and her husband would see Rowe again, but this time at the NCPA for a performance of Beethoven's Ninth. Rowe was one of only five musicians from 1973 who still performed with the orchestra.

Inside the concert hall, Cui and Zhang settled into their seats near the front. Backstage, Yannick, dressed all in black, took a quick swig from a water bottle before striding onstage with a smile. The audience greeted him with rousing applause. The conductor hopped onto the podium and, with a flick of his arms, signaled to the musicians and the Chinese singers arrayed behind them that they should stand to acknowledge the applause. They settled back into their seats, eyes fixed on their conductor.

Yannick stood before the musicians and singers as a stillness descended on the hall like the quiet before a storm. He gently raised his hands.

The music began.

AFTERWORD

March 2020 got off to a hectic start. That first week, we sprinted to finish our documentary *Beethoven in Beijing*—"locking" the final edit, in film parlance—to send it off to the first of many film festivals that had rewarded our effort with an official selection. I looked forward to savoring the moment and exhaling. It had taken five years to turn an idea into a film, and now we could begin sharing the story with audiences across the country.

My husband and I had tickets for the Philadelphia Orchestra at the Kimmel Center and a program that seemed like a serendipitous celebration: a doubleheader of Beethoven's Fifth and Sixth Symphonies, the two works at the center of the dramatic brouhaha between Conductor Eugene Ormandy and Madame Mao during the 1973 tour. The concert would kick off the orchestra's yearlong celebration of Beethoven's 250th birthday. We'd go out to dinner and then take our usual seats in the conductor's circle at 7:30 P.M. on Thursday, March 12.

And then. . . .

Conductor Yannick Nézet-Séguin did perform both masterpieces—before an empty concert hall at the Kimmel Center. A microscopic killer had begun to ravage the country, forcing a stop to public gatherings and the start of a protracted quarantine. I watched the concert on my computer at home. Before the music started, the normally upbeat Yannick, dressed head to toe in black, faced the deserted Verizon Hall and addressed listeners at home. None of us knew what would unfold in the months ahead, but he offered words of comfort. "This music will help us, guide us and channel all our emotions, and help us feel we're together," he assured. And when the evening was over, the musicians rose in their seats and followed Yannick in turning toward the empty house, enveloped in a mournful silence.

That was the last time the musicians performed as a full orchestra that year. But the orchestra adjusted. It created a digital stage and opened its archival vault to present gems from long ago for us to enjoy again at home. It wasn't until August that two dozen string musicians were filmed and streamed from the outdoor stage at the Mann Music Center—six feet apart and with plexiglass partitions. And here, instead of applause, we heard crickets. Heading into the 2020–21 season, the musicians continued performing at the Mann as long as the weather held out, before returning indoors to the stage at the Kimmel Center, albeit digitally and with a smaller ensemble of no more than fifty musicians. Of course, the virtual performances could never match the live concerts in Verizon Hall in impact or emotion, let alone revenue. But, as Yannick told the *Philadelphia Inquirer*, "We're very proud to have kept music alive at a time when people have needed it the most."

The last time I had heard the Philadelphia Orchestra perform Beethoven's Sixth was at the National Centre for the Performing Arts in Beijing during the 2019 tour of China. The full house was enthusiastic, even as relations between the United States and China were fraying. At the time, the two nations were sparring over trade. A few months later, that would seem like a minor dust-up compared to the finger-pointing that erupted when the coronavirus began its deadly spread from the Chinese city of Wuhan.

I filled my days with long-distance interviews and panel discussions at virtual film festivals via Zoom from my attic office. I watched the film's official "premiere," a streaming event watched by thousands of fans aching to hear their beloved orchestra. And I worked on this book, often with Beethoven playing thinly through my computer's speakers.

It was a gentle form of torment, these constant reminders of what we were all missing. I yearned for the full resonance and swelling emotion we experience in a concert hall, shared alongside thousands of like-minded devotees. It is then that we all sense music's undeniable power to lift us above our mortal concerns, to connect us, and to heal. It's as true today as it was in 1973.

ACKNOWLEDGMENTS

When I pitched the idea of a film to the Philadelphia Orchestra, then-CEO Allison Vulgamore suggested that I work with Sam Katz, the founder of History Making Productions (HMP), who has made a second career as a filmmaker mining Philadelphia's history. Because of Sam's support, tenacity, and confidence, we made it through the tortuous, protracted process of bringing an idea to the screen. The HMP team—including codirector Sharon Mullally, editor Rachel Sophia Stewart, director of photography Paul Van Haute, animator Jacob Rivkin, and archival producer Jon Kohl—helped me shape the contours of the film story, which, in turn, serves as a starting point for this written account. Appreciation also goes to Wendy Cox, a veteran producer, who provided me with insight into the film world, candid feedback, moral support, and laughs along the way.

For the film and this book, I am indebted to the musicians who generously gave of their time to recount for me their memories of the 1973 trip. The list is long and includes, but is not limited to, Davyd Booth, Renard Edwards, Larry Grika, Herb Light, Anthony Orlando, and Booker Rowe. The amateur photographers on the trip—among them, the late percussionist Alan Abel, violinist Julia Janson, and orchestra physician Ed Viner—generously shared their images with me.

At the same time, I benefited from the vast scholarship of authors Sheila Melvin and Jindong Cai, who literally wrote the book on classical music in China (three, in fact!) and patiently steered me through the historic and cultural significance of the tour. Without their guidance and encouragement, I could not have written the book or codirected the documentary.

In Beijing, my *lao pengyou* Guo Hui helped me connect with former Central Philharmonic Society musicians, including Cui Zhuping and Zhang Dihe, who kindly invited me into their home. Kaitlin Ryan, executive director of Parnassus Productions, made sure that I connected with composer Tan Dun, whose life story was an essential bridge from 1973 to the present. My translator Mei Chen, meanwhile, patiently guided me through Chinese articles, letters, and correspondences.

I am grateful for the generosity of Mary Planten-Krell, who lent me the personal journal of her uncle, piccolo player John Krell. Diplomat Nicholas Platt also shared the journal of his late wife, Sheila, as well as photographs and hours and hours of his time. I relied on Ambassador Platt's knowledge to place this story in its proper geopolitical context. David Beverage, meanwhile, lent his talent as a graphic artist to show me visually how this oral telling of history could be presented.

My first dive into researching the Philadelphia Orchestra's China legacy started at the Kislak Center for Special Collections, Rare Books and Manuscripts at the University of Pennsylvania, where the staff helped me navigate the extensive archives for Eugene Ormandy. I pored through boxes and boxes of photographs, letters, articles, music scores, and other ephemera about the 1973 China tour, which had been the focus of a special exhibit at the Penn library in 2012. Across town, the archivists at Temple University's Urban Archives pulled from their shelves tattered envelopes filled with all the coverage from the *Philadelphia Bulletin* and the *Philadelphia Inquirer* and helped me comb the collection for TV coverage. Early on, I was fortunate to connect with Kati Marton, the only television reporter to travel with the orchestra. Kati shared her memories and a copy of her Peabody-winning 1973 documentary about the tour, *Overture to Friendship*.

The staff at the Philadelphia Orchestra was essential to the success of the documentary and book. Thank you to Allison Vulgamore for giving us a green light; to Ryan Fleur, executive director, for clearing obstacles; and to current CEO Matias Tarnapolsky for ongoing support. Back in 2015, when I had just the idea for a deeper exploration of the orchestra's China legacy, the first person I pitched was Katherine Blodgett, then the head of public relations, who connected me with Fleur; Tim Kastner, director of digital media; and Craig Hamilton, former head of global initiatives for the orchestra. It took time, but by 2016, we were on our way. My appreciation also goes to other members of the orchestra's administration, including Ashley Berke, vice president of communications; Darrin Britting, publications director; and Jack McCarthy, the orchestra's archival consultant. Former orchestra manager Cathy Barbash, meanwhile, shared with me her insight into cultural diplomacy and an understanding of the orchestra's current approach to engagement in China. Photographers Jan Regan and David Swanson provided essential images for the book.

Finally, in the course of writing this book and finishing the documentary, I relied on the unwavering support of my sisters—Angela, Daria, Damien, and Stefanie—and the "Fam," Bill, Cory, and Karl. Since our days together in the newsroom of the *Pittsburgh Post-Gazette* in the 1980s, Bill has been my partner and personal editor. He's the first person to read a draft and the last. Without him, I would not be writing the final words of this book or celebrating the release of our documentary.

NOTES ON CONTENT

CHAPTER 1: OVERTURE

To place the China tour into the context of music diplomacy, I relied on the insight of historians Sheila Melvin and Jindong Cai, authors of *Rhapsody in Red: How Western Classical Music Became Chinese* (Algora, 2004). When the tour was announced in February 1973, Conductor Eugene Ormandy shared with reporters how he had been lobbying the White House for two years. In particular, Sandy Grady of the *Philadelphia Bulletin* pinpointed that Ormandy had been mulling a tour as far back as April 1971 in a column on September 10, 1973, "Our No. 1 Team Off to China."[1]

CHAPTER 2: WHITE HOUSE CALLING

The conversation between President Richard Nixon, Eugene Ormandy, and National Security Adviser Henry Kissinger was taken from a White House audio recording, released in 2009 by the Nixon Presidential Library.

CHAPTER 3: THE OBVIOUS CHOICE

For this chapter, I interviewed musicians from the 1973 tour—Emilio Gravagno, Alan Abel, Bernard Garfield, Davyd Booth, Margarita Csonka Montanaro, and Larry Grika—over the course of five years, beginning in 2015. Abel, a percussionist for the Philadelphia Orchestra for thirty-eight years and an innovator who designed instruments, succumbed to the COVID-19 virus in April 2020 at the age of ninety-one. He was an accomplished photographer, and, when we first met in 2015, he shared with me hundreds of slides that he took while on tour in China.

---

1. Excerpts from this and other cited *Philadelphia Bulletin* columns by Sandy Grady are reprinted by permission of Spelling Entertainment Group, LLC.

As one of three newspaper reporters on the tour, Daniel Webster, the former music critic for the *Philadelphia Inquirer*, was retired from the paper when I spoke with him at his home in 2015. In addition to material from that interview, I included quotes and observations from his coverage of the tour as well as a first-person account that he wrote for *Playbill* magazine in 2008 on the occasion of the thirty-fifth anniversary of the China tour.

Nicholas Platt and his late wife, Sheila, were key sources for me. Our conversations began in 2008, during the thirty-fifth-anniversary tour of the Philadelphia Orchestra in China, and continued through 2020 at their home in New York City. In addition to our interviews, I also quoted from the former diplomat's memoir, *China Boys: How U.S. Relations with the PRC Began and Grew* (New Academia Publishing/VELLUM Books, 2010).[2]

For Eugene Ormandy's recollection of China, in this chapter and others, I primarily relied on three sources: news coverage of the tour from taken the *Inquirer*, the *Philadelphia Bulletin*, and the *New York Times*; a 1973 Peabody Award–winning documentary produced by WCAU-TV reporter Kati Marton; and an audio recording of a press conference about China held on January 15, 1974, at the National Press Club in Washington, DC.[3]

For the sidebar on the "Fabulous Philadelphians," I consulted *The Philadelphia Orchestra: A Century of Music*, edited by John Adroin (Temple University Press, 1999). The *Philadelphia Inquirer* covered the first concert of the orchestra in an unsigned article on November 17, 1900, under the headline "The Philadelphia Orchestra: It Gave Its First Concert at the Academy of Music Last Evening before a Large and Brilliant Audience."

For a second sidebar on the 1940 China Aid Concert, I consulted John Pomfret's *The Beautiful Country and the Middle Kingdom: America and China, 1776 to the Present* (Henry Holt, 2016) to put the event into the proper historical context.

Chapter 4: *Yellow River* Panic

Cables between the late Francis Tenny, a cultural attaché in Washington, DC, and Nicholas Platt, a political officer in Beijing with the U.S. Liaison Office, were declassified by the U.S. State Department in 2005 and made available online by WikiLeaks in 2013. Some of the quotes from Tenny

---

2. Passages from *China Boys* reprinted by permission of New Academia Publishing.
3. Excerpts from Eugene Ormandy's press conference reprinted by permission of the National Press Club.

came from an online essay that he wrote about the orchestra's tour for *American Diplomacy* that appeared in June 2012.[4]

Ormandy recounted in detail the last-minute performance of Daniel Epstein in Saratoga Springs, New York, at a press luncheon in 1974 at the National Press Club in Washington, DC. In 2020, I interviewed Epstein, a concert pianist and educator who teaches at the Manhattan School of Music, for his recollection of events. Yin Chengzong, the pianist who led the committee that composed the *Yellow River Concerto* and did most of the work, shared with me his reaction to criticism for a profile of him that I wrote for the *Philadelphia Inquirer* on May 30, 2008, on the eve of the thirty-fifth-anniversary concert of the 1973 tour in Beijing.

For the sidebar on the *Yellow River Concerto*, I relied on Yin and the expertise of conductor Jindong Cai and his wife, journalist Sheila Melvin.

CHAPTER 5: SEPTEMBER 10: PIONEERS

During the Philadelphia Orchestra's 2017 tour of China, I caught up with James Barnes, the son of a stagehand, for an interview before a concert, and then I followed up with him in 2020, the year of his retirement. My interview with Edward and Judith Viner, the physician and the nurse on tour, took place at their Philadelphia home in 2019. Dr. Viner, another photographer among the travelers, shared with me his slides from the trip. Booker Rowe, a violinist with the orchestra for forty-nine years and its second Black member, began reminiscing with me about China in 2015 with multiple interviews both on background and, in 2019, on camera for the documentary *Beethoven in Beijing*.

Kati Marton, the former WCAU reporter and an author, provided me with guidance and insight during several conversations, the first in 2015. Marton, the only TV reporter among the 1973 press corps, also shared with me a copy of her Peabody Award–winning documentary, *Overture to Friendship*.

Quotes from the late John Krell, a piccolo player, were gleaned from his journal from the trip, which his family shared with me.[5] All of his observations were taken from that diary. In 2008 and

---

4. Passages from Francis Tenny's "The Philadelphia Orchestra's 1973 China Tour" reprinted by permission of the journal *American Diplomacy*: http://americandiplomacy.web.unc.edu.

5. Passages from John Krell's journal reprinted by permission of Mary E. Planten-Krell.

2015, I interviewed Sheila Platt, who was assigned to help her husband, Nicholas, escort Eugene and Gretel Ormandy through China. The Platt family also shared her China journal with me, which included her observations of the Ormandys and anecdotes about the tour.[6]

For the sidebar on "Globetrotters," I consulted John Adroin's history of the Philadelphia Orchestra as well as the recollections of Philadelphia Orchestra players.

Chapter 6: September 11: *Not My Trumpet Player!*

The *Philadelphia Bulletin* made the daring editorial move of sending its popular sports columnist, the late Sandy Grady, to cover the tour. Grady knew little about classical music but brought a sharp eye, wit, and irreverence to his reporting. All of his passages were taken from his columns.

Chapter 7: September 12: Red Carpet Welcome

Herb Light, a violinist for fifty-six years with the Philadelphia Orchestra, is a natural storyteller. I conducted many interviews with him, in Philadelphia, on tour in China, and finally in front of a camera in 2019 for the documentary.

Eugene Ormandy went into detail about the flap over Beethoven's Sixth Symphony at the National Press Club in 1974. Tenny's comments were taken from the essay he wrote for *American Diplomacy*, while Nicholas and Sheila Platt shared recollections in interviews. Sheila also detailed the debate over Beethoven in her personal journal.

For the sidebar on the history of classical music in China, I again relied on the knowledge of authors Jindong Cai and Sheila Melvin, who, in addition to *Rhapsody in Red*, also wrote *Beethoven in China: How the Great Composer Became an Icon in the People's Republic* (Penguin Group, 2015).

Chapter 8: September 13: Tug of War

Julia Janson, a violinist with the orchestra for thirty-one years, spoke with me about the 1973 tour in 2020. All passages attributed to Louis Hood, the Philadelphia Orchestra public relations director, were taken from his account of the trip that ran in three installments of the orchestra's program

---

6. Excerpts from Sheila Platt's journal reprinted by permission of Nicholas Platt.

in 1973 and were later reprinted as a booklet titled *China Diary*.[7] The *Bulletin*'s Grady recalled his first impressions in "China Trip Is Now a Dream," September 24, 1973, and attempts to question people about Watergate in "Commune Urged for Serenity," September 27, 1973.

For the sidebar on Madame Mao, I was guided by the insight of authors Jindong Cai and Sheila Melvin as well as Nicholas Platt's knowledge of the period.

Chapter 9: September 14: Opening Night

Renard Edwards, a violist who, in 1970, became the first Black musician in the Philadelphia Orchestra, spoke with me many times about the 1973 tour, including during an on-camera interview in 2019. During quarantine, I interviewed the retired violinist Robert de Pasquale, who grew up in the Germantown neighborhood of Philadelphia in a remarkable family of musicians, including three brothers who also belonged to the Philadelphia Orchestra.

The retired Chinese musicians who are cited throughout this oral history were interviewed at a 2016 luncheon in Beijing that reunited six musicians from the Central Philharmonic Society with six veterans of the 1973 tour from the Philadelphia Orchestra. The event was arranged and filmed for the documentary *Beethoven in Beijing*. With Zhang Dihe and his wife, Cui Zhuping, I followed up in 2017 with a visit to their home with a film crew.

Chapter 10: September 15: Turned Tables

Anthony Orlando, a percussionist from Reading, Pennsylvania, who performed for forty-six years with the Philadelphia Orchestra, appears in the documentary *Beethoven in Beijing* and sat for an on-camera interview in 2019. The Central Philharmonic musicians who recalled rehearsing for Eugene Ormandy in 1973—oboist Liu Qi and the late violinist Zhu Gongqi—shared their memories in 2016, during the reunion luncheon with Philadelphia musicians.

The description of the 1973 rehearsal by music critic Harold Schonberg came from his article "They Play Beethoven's 5th: Ormandy Conducts Chinese," *New York Times*, September 16, 1973.

Music historians Jindong Cai and Sheila Melvin provided insight into the treatment of classically trained musicians for the sidebar in this chapter, titled "Bourgeois Targets." Newspaper

---

7. Excerpts from *China Diary* © The Philadelphia Orchestra Association. Reprinted by permission.

accounts of the visit to the Central Philharmonic reported on the musical gifts that were exchanged between the two groups.

CHAPTER 11: SEPTEMBER 16: THE BIG ONE

In 2008, I traveled to the island of Gulangyu in the Fujian Province to interview the pianist Yin Chengzong, a soloist and co-composer of *Yellow River Concerto*. His comment in this section was taken from that interview. The remarks of John Holdridge, the number-two diplomat in the U.S. Liaison Office in Beijing, were published in his memoir, *Crossing the Divide: An Insider's Account of the Normalization of U.S.-China Relations* (Rowman and Littlefield, 1997).[8]

CHAPTER 12: SEPTEMBER 17: NEWS OF THE DAY

Tan Dun, the Oscar- and Grammy-winning composer who wrote the score for the blockbuster *Crouching Tiger, Hidden Dragon*, recounted his memory about hearing the Philadelphia Orchestra over a commune loudspeaker during a 2016 on-camera interview with me at his New York home.

CHAPTER 13: SEPTEMBER 18: FRISBEES AND ACUPUNCTURE

The *Bulletin*'s Sandy Grady wrote about Frisbee-mania in "The 'Great Frisbee Riot' Comes to China," September 18, 1973. The *Inquirer*'s Daniel Webster described acupuncture's popularity in "Eight Musicians Undergo Acupuncture," September 19, 1973.[9]

CHAPTER 14: SEPTEMBER 19: NEXT STOP, SHANGHAI

Chinese coverage of the tour's success included Chen Hsing's article "Friendly Sentiments, Brilliant Performance," *People's Daily*, September 19, 1973; and Hua Ying's account "Friendly, Warm, Bril-

---

8. This and other excerpts from *Crossing the Divide* are reproduced with permission of the Licensor through PLSclear.

9. Excerpts from this and other cited *Philadelphia Inquirer* columns by Daniel Webster are reprinted by permission of the *Philadelphia Inquirer*.

liant," *Guangming Daily*, September 19, 1973. The *Bulletin*'s Sandy Grady recounted his *maotai* night in "Maotai Bout Topples Yanks," September 20, 1973.

Information for the sidebar on Shanghai's musical history can be found in *Rhapsody in Red* by music historians Jindong Cai and Sheila Melvin.

CHAPTER 15: SEPTEMBER 20: SIDEWALK SERENADE

Harold Schonberg described the chance encounter between violinist Robert de Pasquale and a Chinese child in the *New York Times* on September 21, 1973, under the headline "Philadelphians Score 2 Hits in Shanghai." De Pasquale also shared his recollections in interviews with me in 2020.

CHAPTER 16: SEPTEMBER 21: REBELS ON POINTE

I conducted several interviews with Hai-ye Ni, principal cello for the Philadelphia Orchestra and a Shanghai native, who recalled her mother's memory of performing for the Philadelphians as part of the orchestra for a Shanghai ballet company. During the Shanghai leg of the 1973 tour, one of the Chinese musicians who attended one of the concerts was my cousin, Julia Tsien, who, at the time, was a piano accompanist for a lyric opera company. Julia entered the Shanghai Conservatory as a young teen, but her training as a concert pianist was cut short by the Cultural Revolution, and, like the composer Tan Dun, she was sent to the countryside to live on a commune.

CHAPTER 17: SEPTEMBER 22: *YOU YI*, FRIENDSHIP

Steve Bell's comments came from a report he did for the *ABC Evening News* that aired on September 24, 1974.

CHAPTER 18: JANUARY 14, 1974: DOWN WITH BEETHOVEN

John Holdridge's account of the renewed crackdown on Beethoven and classical music came from his memoir, *Crossing the Divide*. He also addressed the matter in a cable to the U.S. State Department. The day the news broke coincided with Eugene Ormandy's press conference at the National Press Club in Washington, DC. Both Nicholas Platt and Francis Tenny recalled the renewed campaign against Western music in their published accounts of the tour. Authors Sheila Melvin and Jindong Cai presented a countertheory on the power struggle behind the scenes in *Rhapsody in Red*.

Music critic Harold Schonberg made his disparaging remarks about the *Yellow River Concerto* in the *New York Times* article "Yin Spoke Only Chinese, Ormandy Only English," October 14, 1973. The *Inquirer*'s Daniel Webster recalled the backlash in a *Playbill* article on the occasion of the thirty-fifth anniversary of the tour, "The Philadelphia Orchestra: Learning Chinese," February 1, 2008.

Chapter 19: Epilogue: Ode to Joy

With a crew from History Making Productions, I covered the Philadelphia Orchestra's 2017 concert at the National Centre for the Performing Arts. During a stop in Shanghai, I interviewed Conductor Yannick Nézet-Séguin. Sheila Melvin and Jindong Cai, coauthors of *Rhapsody in Red*, guided me on what happened after the death of Mao Zedong in 1976 and the revival of interest in classical music in China.

This chapter includes material from interviews for the documentary with Allison Vulgamore, former chief executive of the Philadelphia Orchestra; composer Tan Dun; pianist Lang Lang; principal harpist Elizabeth Hainen; and Chinese musicians Cui Zhuping and Zhang Dihe. David Patrick Stearns, a music critic for the *Philadelphia Inquirer*, described Tan Dun's "The Map" in a review, "A Musical Meeting of East and West," which was published on November 13, 2004.

BIBLIOGRAPHY

Books

Adroin, John, ed. *The Philadelphia Orchestra: A Century of Music*. Philadelphia: Temple University Press, 1999.

Holdridge, John H. *Crossing the Divide: An Insider's Account of the Normalization of U.S.-China Relations*. Lanham, MD: Rowman and Littlefield, 1997.

Melvin, Sheila, and Jindong Cai. *Beethoven in China: How the Great Composer Became an Icon in the People's Republic*. Australia: Penguin Group, 2015.

———. *Rhapsody in Red: How Western Classical Music Became Chinese*. New York: Algora, 2004.

Platt, Nicholas. *China Boys: How U.S. Relations with the PRC Began and Grew*. Washington, DC: New Academia Publishing/VELLUM Books, 2010.

Pomfret, John. *The Beautiful Country and the Middle Kingdom: America and China, 1776 to the Present*. New York: Henry Holt, 2016.

Newspaper Articles, Journals, and Other Publications

Associated Press. "Who, What's Played at Ball Sparks Bit of Controversy." *Evening Sun* (Hanover, PA), January 16, 1973.

Chen, Hsing. "Friendly Sentiments, Brilliant Performance." *People's Daily*, September 19, 1973.

Dobrin, Peter. "Philadelphia Orchestra Declared 'Orchestra of Year' by British Classical Magazine." *Philadelphia Inquirer*, October 6, 2020.

———. "Philadelphia Orchestra Goes Shorter, Smaller and Virtual for the First Part of the 2020–21 Season." *Philadelphia Inquirer*, August 17, 2020.

———. "Philly's Classical Music Season Has Arrived. Let the Experimentation Begin." *Philadelphia Inquirer*, September 27, 2020.

Grady, Sandy. "China Trip Is Now a Dream." *Philadelphia Bulletin*, September 24, 1973.

———. "Chinese Do Things Curiously." *Philadelphia Bulletin*, September 17, 1973.

———. "Chinese Hail Orchestra at Final Concert." *Philadelphia Bulletin*, September 23, 1973.

———. "Chinese Pull Out All Stops to Praise Ormandy's Music." *Philadelphia Bulletin*, September 19, 1973.

———. "Commune Urged for Serenity." *Philadelphia Bulletin*, September 27, 1973.

———. "The 'Great Frisbee Riot' Comes to China." *Philadelphia Bulletin*, September 18, 1973.

———. "Madame Mao Steals the Show; Ormandy Doesn't Seem to Mind." *Philadelphia Bulletin*, September 17, 1973.

———. "Mao Ads Saturate Peking." *Philadelphia Bulletin*, September 13, 1973.

———. "Mao-tai Bout Topples Yanks." *Philadelphia Bulletin*, September 20, 1973.

———. "Musical Elite of Peking Welcome Phila. Orchestra in China Visit." *Philadelphia Bulletin*, September 12, 1973.

———. "Never Has My Orchestra Been This Happy. Nothing Would Have Stopped Me from This. Nothing." *Philadelphia Bulletin*, November 4, 1973.

———. "Orchestra's Journey to China Is as Scrutable as Chow Mein." *Philadelphia Bulletin*, September 9, 1973.

———. "Our No. 1 Team off to China." *Philadelphia Bulletin*, September 10, 1973.

———. "Shanghai Rolls Out Carpet for Orchestra." *Philadelphia Bulletin*, September 21, 1973.

———. "Sousa Is the Match: Ormandy Ignites the Chinese." *Philadelphia Bulletin*, September 16, 1973.

Hood, Louis. "China Diary," originally appeared in 1973 as three installments in the Philadelphia Orchestra's program; later reprinted as a booklet.

Hua, Ying. "Friendly, Warm, Brilliant." *Guangming Daily*, September 19, 1973.

Krell, John. Personal journal from Sept. 10–23, 1973.

Lin, Jennifer. "Orchestra Plays It Again, to a Warmer Reception." *Philadelphia Inquirer*, June 3, 2008.

———. "Philadelphia Orchestra Returns to China." *Philadelphia Inquirer*, May 30, 2008.

"The Philadelphia Orchestra: It Gave Its First Concert at the Academy of Music Last Evening before a Large and Brilliant Audience." *Philadelphia Inquirer*, November 17, 1900.

Platt, Sheila. *The Granny Chronicles*, vol. 1. Self-published journal.

Schonberg, Harold. "Ormandy, Unexpectedly, Leads Peking Orchestra." *New York Times*, September 16, 1973.

———. "Philadelphians Score 2 Hits in Shanghai." *New York Times*, September 21, 1973.

———. "Yin Spoke Only Chinese, Ormandy Only English." *New York Times*, October 14, 1973.

Stearns, David Patrick. "A Musical Meeting of East and West." *Philadelphia Inquirer*, November 13, 2004.

———. "Philadelphia Orchestra Ends Its Contentious Israel Tour with a Jerusalem Concert, and Some Soul Searching." *Philadelphia Inquirer*, June 5, 2018.

Tenny, Francis. "The Philadelphia Orchestra's 1973 China Tour," *American Diplomacy*, June 2012. http://americandiplomacy.web.unc.edu/2012/06/the-philadelphia-orchestras-1973-china-tour/.

Webster, Daniel. "Eight Musicians Undergo Acupuncture." *Philadelphia Inquirer*, September 19, 1973.

———. "Even the Orchestra Couldn't Save Beethoven." *Philadelphia Inquirer*, October 3, 1974.

———. "Exploring the Realm of Myth That Is China: The Philadelphia Orchestra Went to China to Play and Also to Learn." *Philadelphia Inquirer*, September 30, 1973.

———. "The Greatest Tour Ever: Orchestra's Visit Ends with an Ovation." *Philadelphia Inquirer*, September 22, 1973.

———. "Mao's Wife Praises Ormandy in Peking." *Philadelphia Inquirer*, September 17, 1973.

———. "Orchestra Greeted Warmly in Peking." *Philadelphia Inquirer*, September 13, 1973.

———. "Orchestra Is Cheered by Thousands Lining Route into Shanghai." *Philadelphia Inquirer*, September 20, 1973.

———. "Orchestra Will Tour China This Year." *Philadelphia Inquirer*, February 23, 1973.

———. "The Philadelphia Orchestra: Learning Chinese." *Playbill*, February 1, 2008.

Williams, Edgar. "Police, Fire Band Sends Orchestra off to Red China." *Philadelphia Inquirer*, September 11, 1973.

Xinhua News Agency. "Philadelphia Orchestra of U.S. Welcomed at Peking Banquet." September 13, 1973.

———. "U.S. Philadelphia Orchestra Group Performs in Peking." September 17, 1973.

VIDEO AND AUDIO ARCHIVES

ABC News. Television newscast. Steve Bell, September 27, 1973.

Library of Congress. National Press Club collection preservation tape RXA 1477, January 15, 1974.

Richard Nixon Presidential Library. Audio recording of phone call from President Nixon and Henry Kissinger to Eugene Ormandy, February 20, 1973. Conversation No. 43–124.

DIPLOMATIC CABLES

U.S. Liaison Office Peking. "Music and Class Struggle." Wikileaks Cable: 1974PEKING00101_b. Dated Jan. 17, 1974. https://wikileaks.org/plusd/cables/1974PEKING00101_b.html.

———. "Philadelphia Orchestra." Wikileaks Cable: 1973PEKING00645_b. Dated July 25, 1973. https://wikileaks.org/plusd/cables/1973PEKING00645_b.html.

———. "Philadelphia Orchestra." Wikileaks Cable: 1973PEKING01050_b. Dated September 15, 1973. https://wikileaks.org/plusd/cables/1973PEKING01050_b.html.

———. "Philadelphia Orchestra." Wikileaks Cable: 1973PEKING01065_b. Dated September 17, 1973. https://wikileaks.org/plusd/cables/1973PEKING01065_b.html.

U.S. State Department. "Philadelphia Orchestra." Wikileaks Cable: 1973STATE142576_b. Dated July 20, 1973. https://wikileaks.org/plusd/cables/1973STATE142576_b.html.

———. "Philadelphia Orchestra." Wikileaks Cable: 1973STATE170461_b. Dated August 27, 1973. https://wikileaks.org/plusd/cables/1973STATE170461_b.html.

———. "Philadelphia Orchestra." Wikileaks Cable: 1973STATE175778_b. Dated September 4, 1973. https://wikileaks.org/plusd/cables/1973STATE175778_b.html.

———. "Philadelphia Orchestra." Wikileaks Cable: 1973STATE176475_b. Dated September 5, 1973. https://wikileaks.org/plusd/cables/1973STATE176475_b.html.

INDEX

Page numbers in *italics* refer to photographs.

JENNIFER LIN is an award-winning journalist, author, and documentary filmmaker. She created and codirected the feature-length documentary, *Beethoven in Beijing*, which premiered on PBS's *Great Performances* in 2021. For 31 years, she worked at the *Philadelphia Inquirer* as a reporter, including posts as a foreign correspondent in China, a financial correspondent on Wall Street, and a national correspondent in Washington, DC. She is the author of *Shanghai Faithful: Betrayal and Forgiveness in a Chinese Christian Family* and coauthor of *Sole Sisters: Stories of Women and Running*.